CHRISTIAN COIGNY

SITTINGS

VICKI GOLDBERG

RAY EAMES
NIGEL KENNEDY
TOURÉ KUNDA
SONNY ROLLINS
DIZZY GILLESPIE
MILES DAVIS
JOHN CAGE
LOU REED
LAURIE ANDERSON
LUCIANO DE CRESCENZO
JOHN LURIE
CASSANDRA WILSON
MARTIN SCORSESE
PHILIP JOHNSON
JEAN NOUVEL
CHRISTIAN DE PORTZAMPARC
ETTORE SOTTSASS
FRANK O. GEHRY
ISSEY MIYAKE
FRANCO MOSCHINO
PETER GREENAWAY
FRANK STELLA
ELLSWORTH KELLY
TOM WESSELMAN
ROY LICHTENSTEIN
JAMES ROSENQUIST
ROBERT RYMAN
ROBERT WILSON
GILBERT AND GEORGE
KEITH HARING
JEFF KOONS
JEAN TINGUELY
JÖRG IMMENDORFF
JIM DINE
LOUISE BOURGEOIS
ARNULF RAINER
JEAN-LUC GODARD
GEORG BASELITZ
JASPER JOHNS
DAVID HOCKNEY
MERCE CUNNINGHAM
PINA BAUSCH
MARCIA HAYDÉE
MAURICE BÉJART
MIKHAIL BARYSHNIKOV
SIMON WIESENTHAL
ALLEN GINSBERG
JEAN BAUDRILLARD
CHARLES BUKOWSKI
PATRICIA HIGHSMITH
WILLIAM BURROUGHS
JOHN UPDIKE
VOLKER SCHLÖNDORFF
JACK LEMMON
MICHEL PICCOLI
FRANCIS FORD COPPOLA
SPIKE LEE
WIM WENDERS
GIULETTA MASINA
ROMAN POLANSKI
JOHN MALKOVICH
HANNA SCHYGULLA
PETER BROOK
BILLY WILDER
LAUREN BACALL
DENNIS HOPPER
JEANNE MOREAU
BEN KINGSLEY
PEDRO ALMODÓVAR
GRACE JONES
AUDREY HEPBURN
HELMUT NEWTON
DAVID COPPERFIELD
ADAIR RED
LINFORD CHRISTIE
BARBARA HENDRICKS
GIORGIO GIUGIARO
JEAN MARAIS
DANIEL BARENBOIM
ALI AKBAR KHAN
GEORGE SEGAL
MILOS FORMAN
RINGO STARR
DOUG TOMPKINS
ROBERT RAUSCHENBERG
GIORGIO STREHLER
TOMI UNGERER
JERRY LEWIS
JOHN BALDESSARI
LEO CASTELLI
ED KOCH
JULIA MIGENES
ISABELLE HUPPERT
VICTOR KORCHNOI
JOHN IRVING
ALAIN DELON
SIMON ESTES
LUCIANO BENETTON
ALEXANDRE TRAUNER
GARRY KASPAROV
OLEG POPOV
ZINO DAVIDOFF
ANTONIO GADES
GIL EVANS
PHIL COLLINS
STING
PHILIP GLASS
YEHUDI MENUHIN
DANIEL SPOERRI
VAKLAV HAVEL
CLAES OLDENBURG
COOSJE VAN BRUGGEN
HUGO PRATT
JAN HOET
REINHOLD MESSNER
ANTONI TÀPIES
BARBARA KRUGER
KRONOS QUARTET
MARGARETE MITSCHERLICH

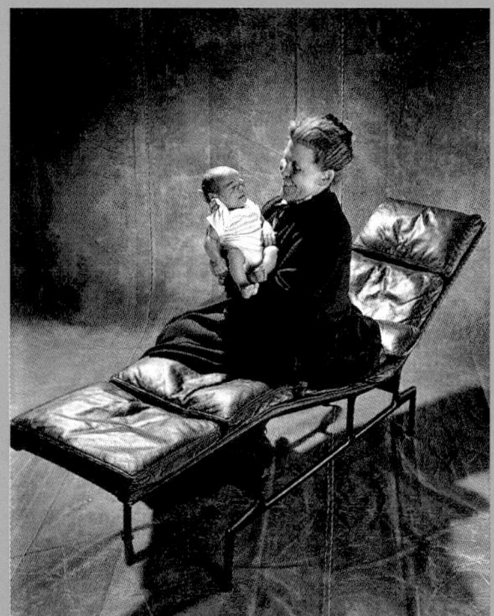

Ray Eames and great-granddaughter
on Eames chaise lounge.

Foreword

Imagine you could form a club and succeed in convincing your heroes, and others you are curious about, to join as members. This was more or less the scenario when we launched the "Personalities on Vitra Chairs" project. Miles Davis, Jasper Johns, John Cage, Robert Rauschenberg, and many others joined over the years. The common denominator was that at some point between 1987 and 1997 every member of our "club" spent a short time sitting for a portrait by photographer Christian Coigny on a Vitra chair.

The project was our response to the standard approach to advertisement in the trade, usually an appealing girl in a short skirt, attractively posed on a chair, juxtaposed with copy full of pseudo-medical and ergonomical jargon. In 1987, Heini Weber and Etienne Aebi showed me a newspaper photograph of Henry Kissinger on a Vitra chair (a photomontage). They suggested that we make a book with portraits of famous people seated on our chairs. To begin with, the photographs—denoted only by the name of the person and the name of the chair—could appear as ads in selected magazines.

Henry wasn't available and, at any rate, he didn't belong to the category of public figures in which we were interested. Our aim was to seek out people one would never associate with advertising of any kind, and whom we would be able to meet in this manner—although I never did use the opportunity of meeting any of them and wasn't present at the photo shoots.

Photographer Christian Coigny, who had just published a book entitled *Portrait d'Artistes*, was recommended for the project. When he succeeded in gaining Godard for the first portrait on the strength of personal acquaintance, the project was up and running. Naturally, Godard had not thought of himself as an advertising vehicle, and neither his facial expression nor his body language could be taken as an invitation to buy the Vitra chair on which he was photographed. Nor was there any attempt to create an illusion that the chair might be his. The chair was simply a prop.

The reaction to these images in magazines was "Who's that?" or "How did 'X' come to sit on this chair?" The public was surprised and at times amused. That's all we wanted to achieve. I pursued the project with a collector's passion. How many of those on our wish list could we entice into the imaginary club? The more people who agreed the easier it became, and when we passed the one hundred mark, the game began to lose its appeal. In the meantime, advertising with real people not associated with the medium had become a trend. It was time to bring the project to conclusion and to realize the book that had sparked it in the first place. The last portraits were taken in 1997.

While the club was a very fluid concept, one personal relationship did emerge from these years, our relationship with Christian Coigny. We awaited each set of prints with bated breath and tremendous excitement. His sensitivity invariably enabled him to discover the real person within the public figure. How would he manage the balancing act this time and what joy, or misery, had the encounter cost him? And speaking of misery, this project earned me the worst fight of my life, with Richard Serra, who accused me of exploiting artists. At Donati's, a restaurant in Basel, glasses flew through the air and one name was crossed off the wish list.

Rolf Fehlbaum
Vitra CEO

Sitting Pretty

Vicki Goldberg

These are photographs of people on chairs and of chairs with people on them, but they are about other things, too. They are about design, and one particular design company. They are also about fame, the relationship of fame to consumerism, and the relationship of portraiture to fame. They are about selling and the construction of prestige and desire, which is to say they are about the nature of advertising. This may seem like a lot of folderol to load onto what are essentially intelligent and entertaining commercial portraits of contemporary celebrities, but philosophy has recently decreed that the unexamined picture is not worth viewing, and Christian Coigny's portraits of people and chairs for Vitra invite viewing on several scores.

They fulfill several functions. As the subjects are celebrities, their portraits should acknowledge and comment on their individuality and/or fame. That is a requirement of all celebrity portraiture, which in our day has been made more difficult (when it hasn't been made boring or outrageous) by the ceaseless proliferation of celebrities and pictures of them. An extra dimension is tacked on in this case: the reputation must be large enough in fact and in appearance to lend distinction to the chair.

The sitters here are mostly singers, actors, directors, and creative types like artists, architects, and writers, important categories in an era so dependent on widespread communications. Certainly the features of those in the entertainment world are expected to be well known. (Although if you are as innocent, as un-hip, as out of it as I, your self-respect could suffer in the face of so many stars you do not recognize without reading their names.)

Christian Coigny says that since the people were all more famous than he, the assignment was a lesson in humility. The rest of us are not supposed to react that way. It must be perfectly clear that these people are worth my attention, and ideally I must think them *interesting* enough for the chair to acquire some measure of interest as well, as if the sitter were radiating importance to the nearest object at hand.

Another piece of extra baggage for the photographer: everyone, or virtually everyone, must be seated. Even in the nineteenth century, when exposures were so long that people's heads were fastened into iron headstands to keep them still, portrait studios sometimes allowed subjects to stand with a steadying hand on a table or column and sometimes took only bust-length portraits. It is a tribute to Coigny that these hundred-odd pictures achieve a certain amount of variety without undue strain or convolution.

His means were relatively simple, his exposures relatively long (1/5 or 1/8 of a second). He threw in a lot of light behind people, bestowing haloes on some. A piece of rather tatty cloth often covers parts of the background and languidly drapes the wall or spreads its folds across floors and walls and even once or twice across feet. The cloth, a useful disguise in hotel bedrooms or conference rooms where the famous were housed for the night, is a distant descendant of the fraying rugs Irving Penn once pitted celebrities against. Coigny's cloth, like Penn's carpet, reminds the viewer of the artifice involved in picture making and forces the subjects to assert themselves without benefit of the kindly support of interior decor.

Celebrities seldom want to give the photographer a lot of their precious time and are anyway a little tired of the whole enterprise before they begin. They probably come prepared with a public face and persona and either have no intention of going beyond that or no longer have any beyond to go to. Coigny says he had ten to thirty minutes for these pictures, with an average of fifteen. Daniel Barenboim gave him seven. Martin Scorsese had something like five press conferences to get to that day. Grace Jones didn't even turn up for her appointment the first three times.

He wanted to grab something intimate, wanted to penetrate, even a little, the personality in front of his lens. Not easy to do at best. What's more, Coigny says that he's very shy and never speaks when photographing. (He adds that he learned a lot about himself taking these portraits—but is still as shy as he used to be.) So: no time to warm the subject up, learn something about him (or her), get him to drop his guard. Coigny likes a little distance, however, likes to watch the subjects for a couple of minutes, see how they move, make a snap decision in what he himself calls "a very artificial way" about what they are and what makes them tick and then try to capture that.

He didn't direct the poses but let the sitter sit. At times, though, he had the feeling they were challenging him to see how he'd manage to get something out of them. A few of them were awkward with the chair. Some would get too comfortable, sit back, and cross their legs, which the photographer considered the worst thing that could happen to him because it was the most boring pose. Then he would have to do something to make them move.

There is a question as to how much any photograph can capture personality, a fraction of a second being so little of a person's life and experience. Then there's the question of whether a photographer's intervention obscures the true character of the sitter in favor of the photographer's imposed ideas. But great portraits have been made in no time at all, and a photographer might just coax a sitter out of the stiffness that attends the presence of a camera. When J.P. Morgan came to sit for Edward Steichen, Steichen had the pose all worked out and took the picture in an instant. Morgan then said he was uncomfortable, and Steichen suggested he try a more agreeable position. The financier swung around and put himself back into the exact same posture, this time of his own volition. Steichen immediately took a second picture that became a landmark in photographic history. He bade Mr. Morgan good-bye. Total time: three minutes.

It's impossible to know whether Coigny has judged his sitters correctly, but certainly some of his pictures answer expectations or present intriguing evidence. Peter Brook balances precariously but remains in control. Pedro Almodóvar is thoughtful and perhaps a trace amused. Robert Wilson postures elegantly. Jeff Koons plays games. Ettore Sottsass is half Rodin's *Thinker* and half geometric form in a postmodern chair that he designed. Of course a lot of these people come armored in their established images. Spike Lee would lose his movie pass if he wore anything other than a T-shirt and a sour puss. Gilbert and George long ago forgot how to bend any parts of their bodies.

These pictures are about chairs, too. Chairs are not common subjects for artists, not primary subjects anyway. Of course they have played important roles in portrait painting and photography, but those were supporting roles. Groups of chairs, even solitary chairs, have occasionally been known to intrigue photographers. Henri Cartier-Bresson snapped some, and Robert Frank's Paris chairs won a prize from *Life's* Young Photographers' Contest in 1951. Peter Hujar liked chairs a lot, but only if they were in ruinous condition. Artists give a nod to unoccupied chairs from time to time: Van Gogh famously painted a lone chair, Lucas Samaras has fashioned many (some bristling with pins, decidedly not for sitting on), Scott Burton also made many, some forbidding, others decidedly for sitting on. Joel Snyder's are not sittable. Robert Wilson's sometimes hang from the ceiling.

Most of us think of chairs as furniture, essential furniture, but only that. They did not enter history in that guise. For a long while they were for rulers and dignitaries alone. Ordinary people sat on stools or benches, or stood, but English kings have for centuries been crowned in a chair made for Edward I late in the thirteenth century, and lords had seigneurial chairs. Even today, a bishop at his investiture takes his chair, as a chairman or chairwoman does at a meeting. Not until the sixteenth century were chairs produced in any quantity and put to wider use by those who could afford them.

They were soon common enough to be designed and redesigned to accommodate wide skirts, ample flounces, and other changing fashions. The design of chairs to preserve the physical well-being of chair sitters is a more recent development, stemming from the more recent awareness that the sedentary position occupies more and more of less and less healthy lives.

In the twentieth century, designers endowed the chair with unprecedented variety. The fourteenth edition of the *Encyclopedia Britannica*, published in 1929, says that "Chippendale and Hepplewhite between them determined what appears to be the final form of the chair, for since their time practically no new type has lasted, and in its main characteristics the chair of the 20th century is the direct derivative of that of the later 18th." What could the editors of this awesome *omnium gatherum* know about Mies Van der Rohe, Marcel Breuer, Gerrit Rietveld, Eero Saarinen, Charles Eames, Frank Gehry, or even the butterfly chair?

The Vitra chairs no longer signify royalty or authority. And yet in a way they do. Status, anyway. In democratic cultures where kings have been abolished or sidelined, everyone dreams of being or competes to become king or queen of something or other—CEO, richest kid on the block, Pulitzer Prize winner. The position no longer comes with a crown and ermine-trimmed robes, so other signs are devised to indicate position, or yearning for it—signs that supposedly signal achievement, or more than has been achieved, or at least movement in the right direction. In the consumer society, where objects and "life styles" assuage certain lacks, good taste, always an indication of class, has become a substitute for actual status.

Vitra is a classy and very up-to-date design firm. It supports a museum of contemporary furniture and commissioned the building for it from Frank Gehry in 1989. The choice of Vitra chairs is of course supposed to mark the chooser as also classy and up-to-date. The images of the classy guys, and a few classy girls, on these pages were all taken by Coigny for advertisements that ran in upscale publications like *Domus* and *Der Spiegel* in Europe. They work on the principle of gilt by association. The subjects of these portraits are all 24 carat. They have reached the purest states of achievement, and they are sitting on Vitra chairs. Vitra chairs are evidently a symbol of success, or at least of the good taste of achievers. If you can't sing like Lou Reed or write like John Updike, you can still rest your bottom where they rest theirs.

The artistic bent and breadth of creativity in this list lend weight to Vitra's image as an artistically creative design firm. Politicians and world leaders are scarce here; so are financiers and real estate moguls. There is only one sports hero. (And though the cast is international, there are not many blacks or Hispanics, no Asians, relatively few women. Which is not a reflection on the company but rather on the nature of the fields surveyed. Movie directors in Europe and the States, for instance, are more likely to be white males than they are other races or another gender.)

In the long history of portraiture, portraits like these "chair portraits" amount to an invention of rather recent vintage. Portraits were originally of the powerful and then of the well-placed and well-to-do. By the middle of the nineteenth century, photography had bestowed the gift of portraiture on the middle class. The medium, which could widely disseminate the images of the people most admired and desired by the masses, also contributed heavily to the creation and expansion of celebrity as a well-placed class of its own.[i] Not till the end of that century, as advertising expanded, did the celebrity endorsement portrait raise its head, so to speak, and then only in the most limited way. By the second decade of the twentieth century, movie stars had begun, barely, to enter the fray, but things really got going in the 1920s, when advertisers finally made heavy use of photographs, and socialites and a few celebrities lent their faces to cold creams and dinner ware. The celebrity portrait itself was off and running and reached its first climax in the 1930s with Hollywood studio portraiture and magazines like *Vanity Fair*.

The endorsement portrait taken with the object endorsed (as opposed to an endorsement portrait on a page with separate pictures of products existing in a kind of separate reality) is the real innovation, essentially unprecedented in portrait painting. Furniture and professional or symbolic apparatus are common enough, but they are merely props or clues. Pictures like those on these pages make the hierarchy between human beings and objects rather tenuous. Since humans find other humans more intensely interesting than almost any inanimate object other than, say, guns pointed at them or money offered them, the sitters do upstage the chairs. And yet the *intent* of the portraits is to glorify the chairs (and their manufacturer) as much as the sitters.

These are dual portraits, a form common enough among married couples, fairly common among siblings, and not entirely uncommon among people with cherished dogs or horses. (The dogs and horses attract attention and may even be the more beautiful individuals portrayed but are nonetheless tacitly granted secondary status.) The closest type is the travel picture of someone paired with a monument. Most are not really portraits but pictures of the Eiffel Tower or the Sphinx with the best beloved in miniature before it, though when the beloved is up close and the monument distant or partial you could call it a portrait *en passant*. (Tseng Kwong Chi traveled around the world photographing himself in a Mao suit before a multitude of important sites, wreaking havoc on this cliché.) The monument confirms the pilgrimage to it, thereby adding to the worldliness of the person in the picture, but the person confers no status on the monument.

With the sitters of *Sittings*, the object supports the person in more ways than one, and the person's reputation supports the object in return. On the other hand, the object is elevated not to human status but to a centrality that very rarely accrues to objects in portraits. At the same time, even as the sitter is rendered in all his (or her) individuality of feature and style by the photographer's skill, he is also commodified, reduced to the size and nature of his particular celebrity. Celebrity in the sense of reputation is immaterial, an abstraction, more a thing than a human being, and fungible in a way that humans are not.

Celebrity portraits in general operate on this level, the reputation to a certain degree replacing the person represented. But except in fashion shots, where the object-clothing is a bit more tightly tied to the persona, or in a few symbolic portraits like Arnold Newman's of Stravinsky, where the piano lid boldly hogs the space, the design, and the drama, portraits seldom require the famous to share the stage with a prop of almost equal interest. Even such pictures as Penn's of people isolated with a worm-eaten rug, settings that demand attention even more imperiously than the velvet drapes and marble columns and wealthy trappings of baroque portraiture, make clear that the *mise en scène* is designed to reveal the personality rather than the personality meant to reveal the nature of the prop.

Do Coigny's portraits stand (or sit) on their own? Most of them work quite well as celebrity portraits and some work better than that, and they deftly balance the demands made on them—they're nice pictures of the chairs, too. It was of course in Vitra's interest to have arresting pictures as well as cynosure subjects. Ever since the 1920s, when the power of photography to spur dream and desire became clear to many people, advertisers have sought out photographers with multiple skills like Steichen, Paul Outerbridge, Penn, Avedon, Annie Leibovitz. The line between art and commercial photography is almost too thin to discern these days as advertisers beg, borrow, or steal the styles of photographers who are not ordinarily in their camp, from Duane Michals to Barbara Kasten to William Wegman.

Any commercial portrait must satisfy the client (in this case Vitra), probably the sitter, and certainly the photographer, who may or may not have a sense of responsibility to the subject. Coigny himself is inclined to philosophical inquiries and doubts. "A portrait," he says, "is a big problem of conscience." He believes that most of the approaches that showcase the photographer's skill at deploying aesthetics or drama or beauty or originality or shock are big lies that have little to do with the subjects. Even black and white is dishonest, he says: "It's not reality." These are serious charges, and he is entirely serious about them. He has given up photographing for about the last two years to ask himself what it really means and whether photographers are being honest with themselves.

Which doesn't even consider the question of whether the advertiser is being honest with us, or whether the sitters were being honest with the photographer, or with themselves, for that matter. Almost everyone, famous or not, has a camera face that may have little to do with the faces put on for daily wear. And as for reality, we're not supposed to believe in that any more, now that digitization has created so many unreal possibilities. Might as well stick with photography for a while; at least it's fun to look at.

[1] For a fuller discussion, see Vicki Goldberg, *The Power of Photography: How Photographs Changed Our Lives* (New York: Abbeville Press, 1991), pp. 103–105.

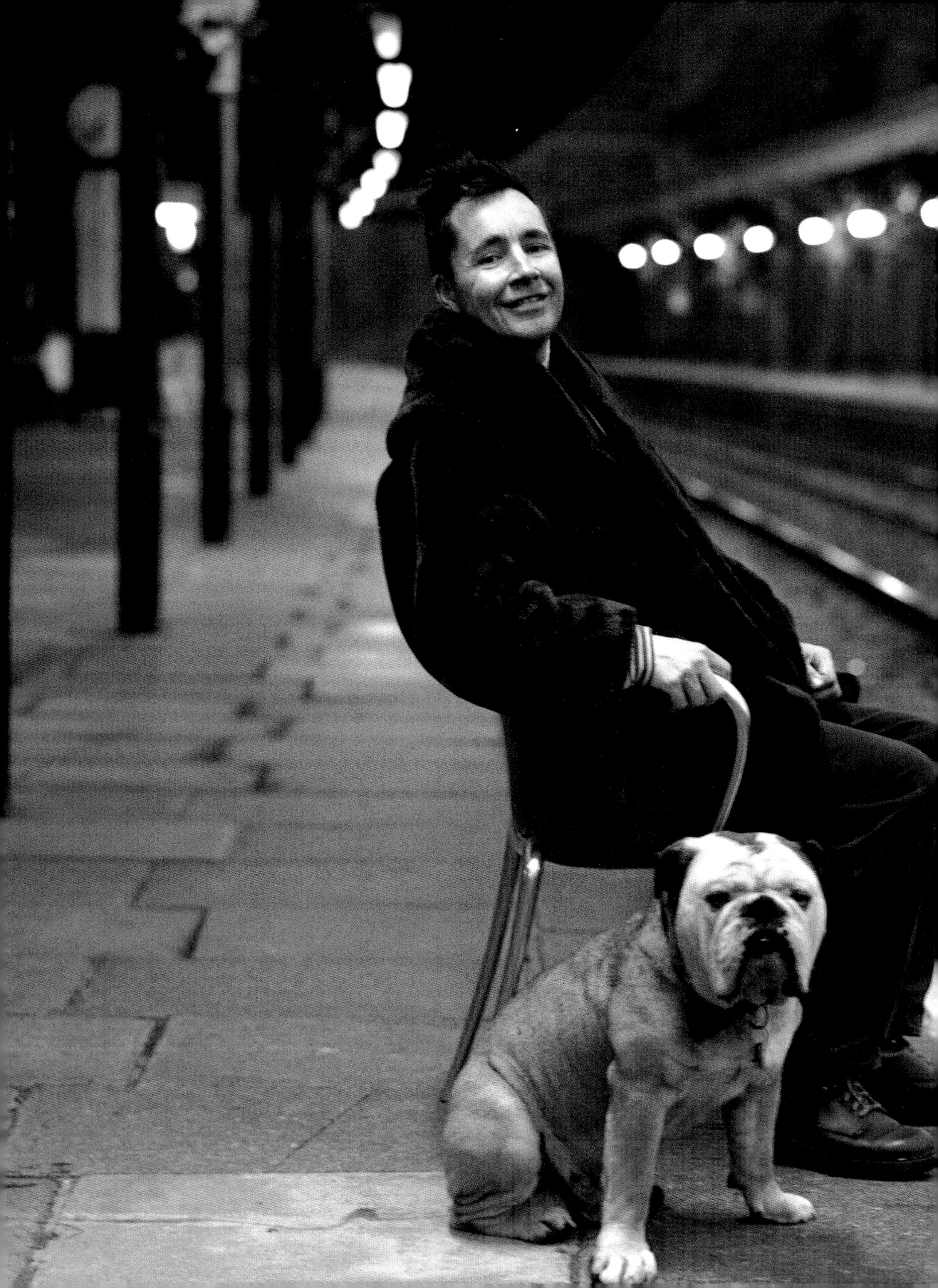

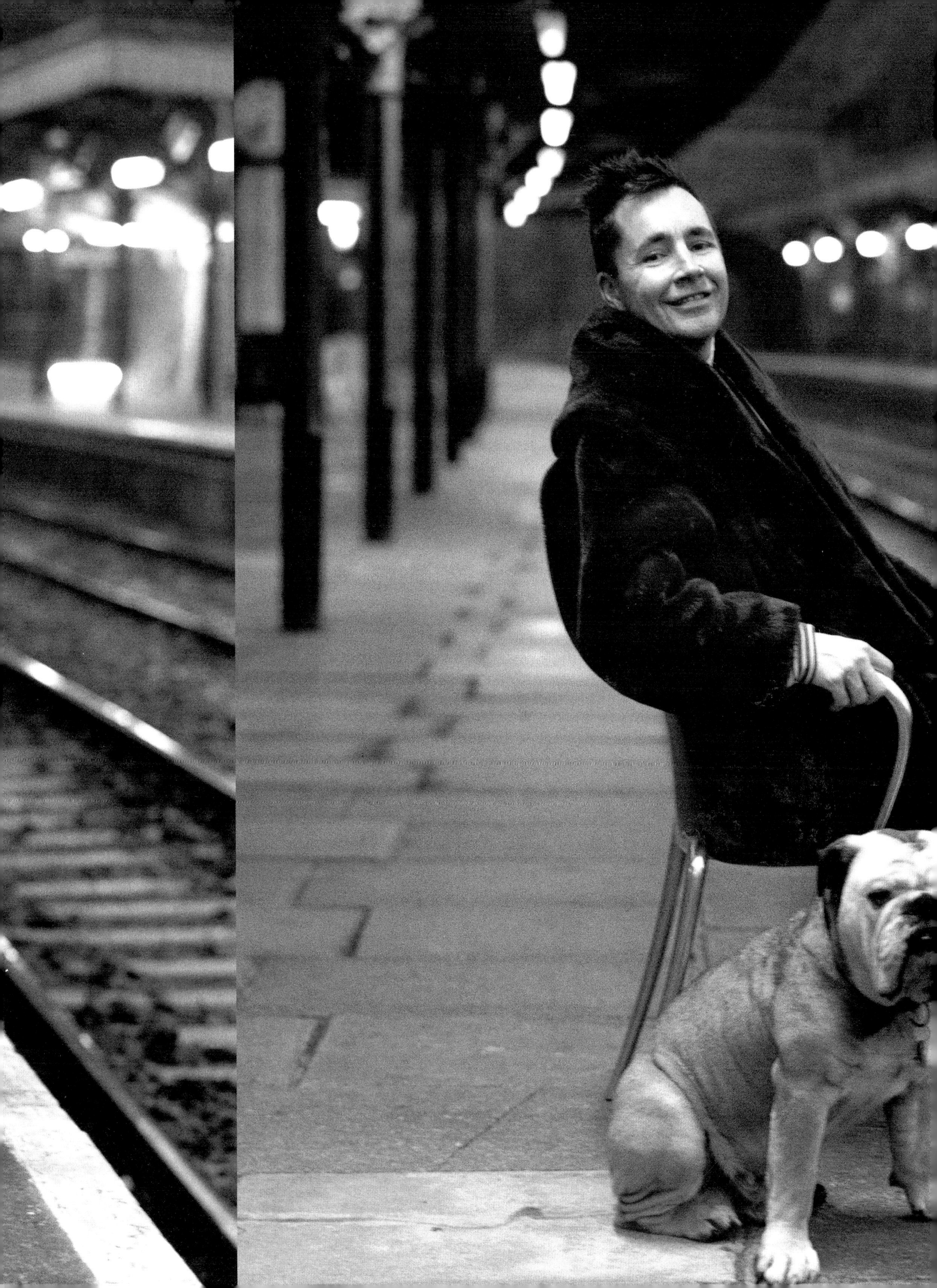

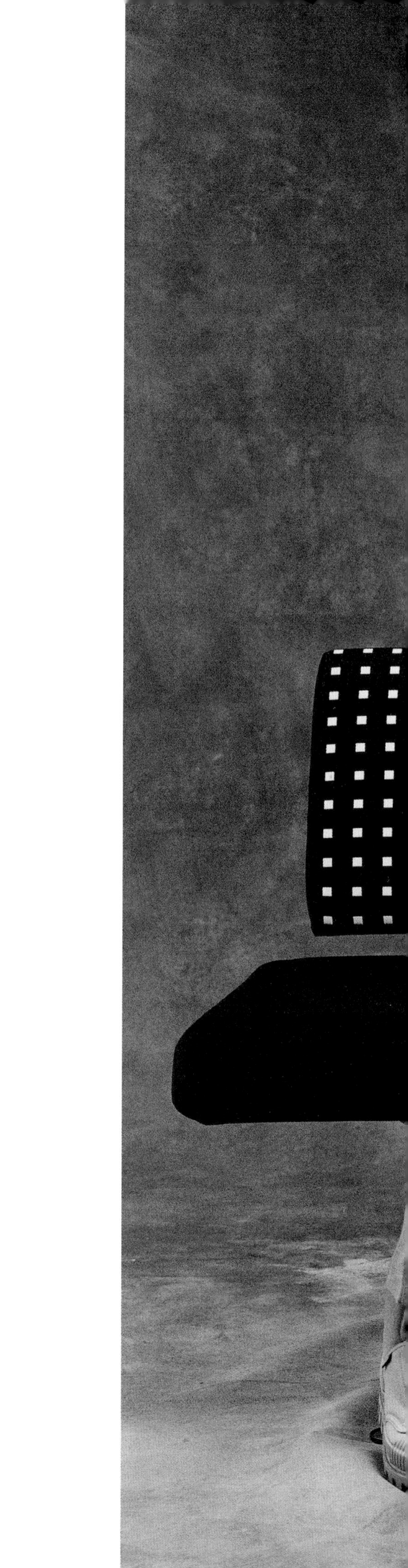

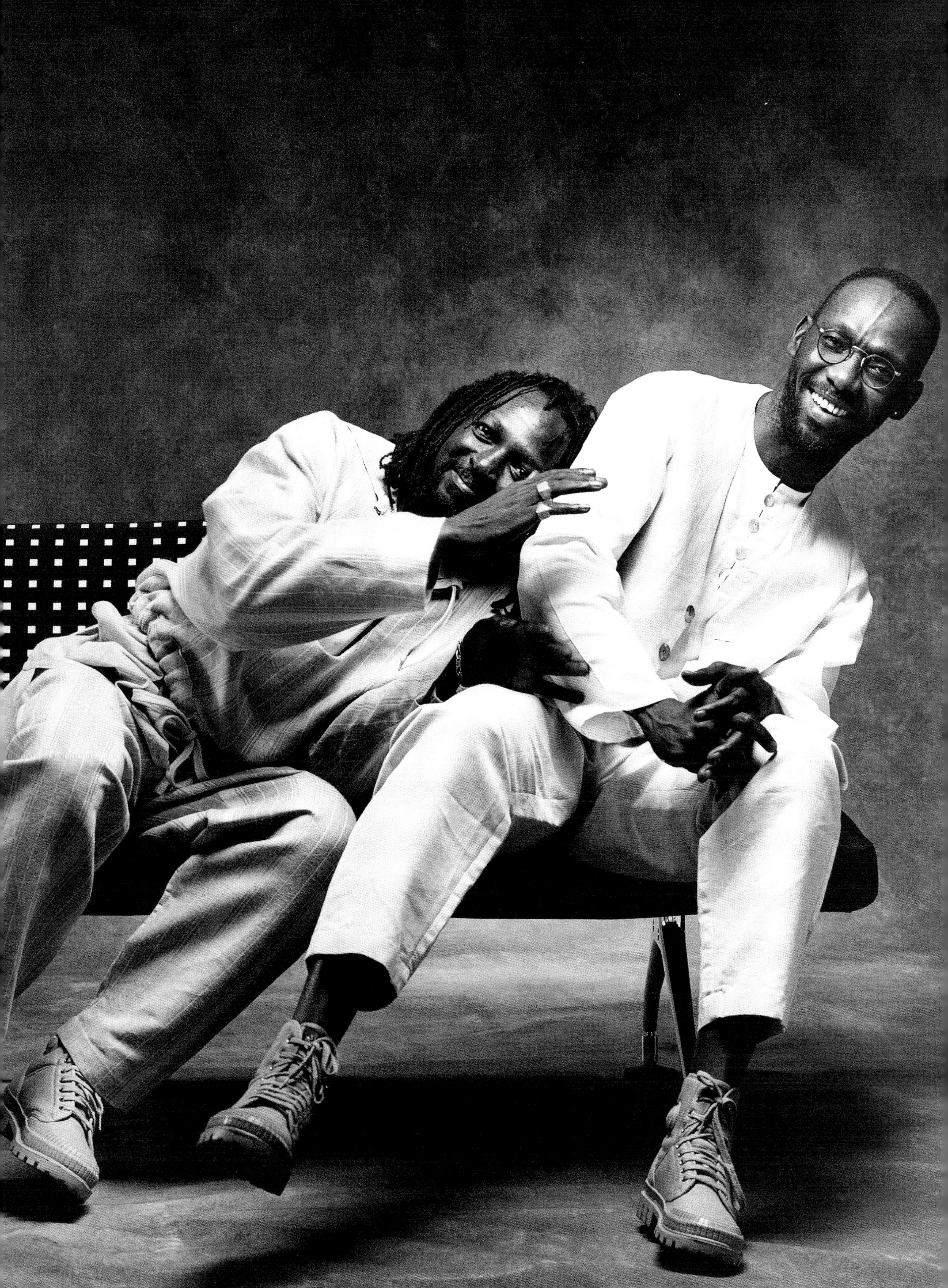

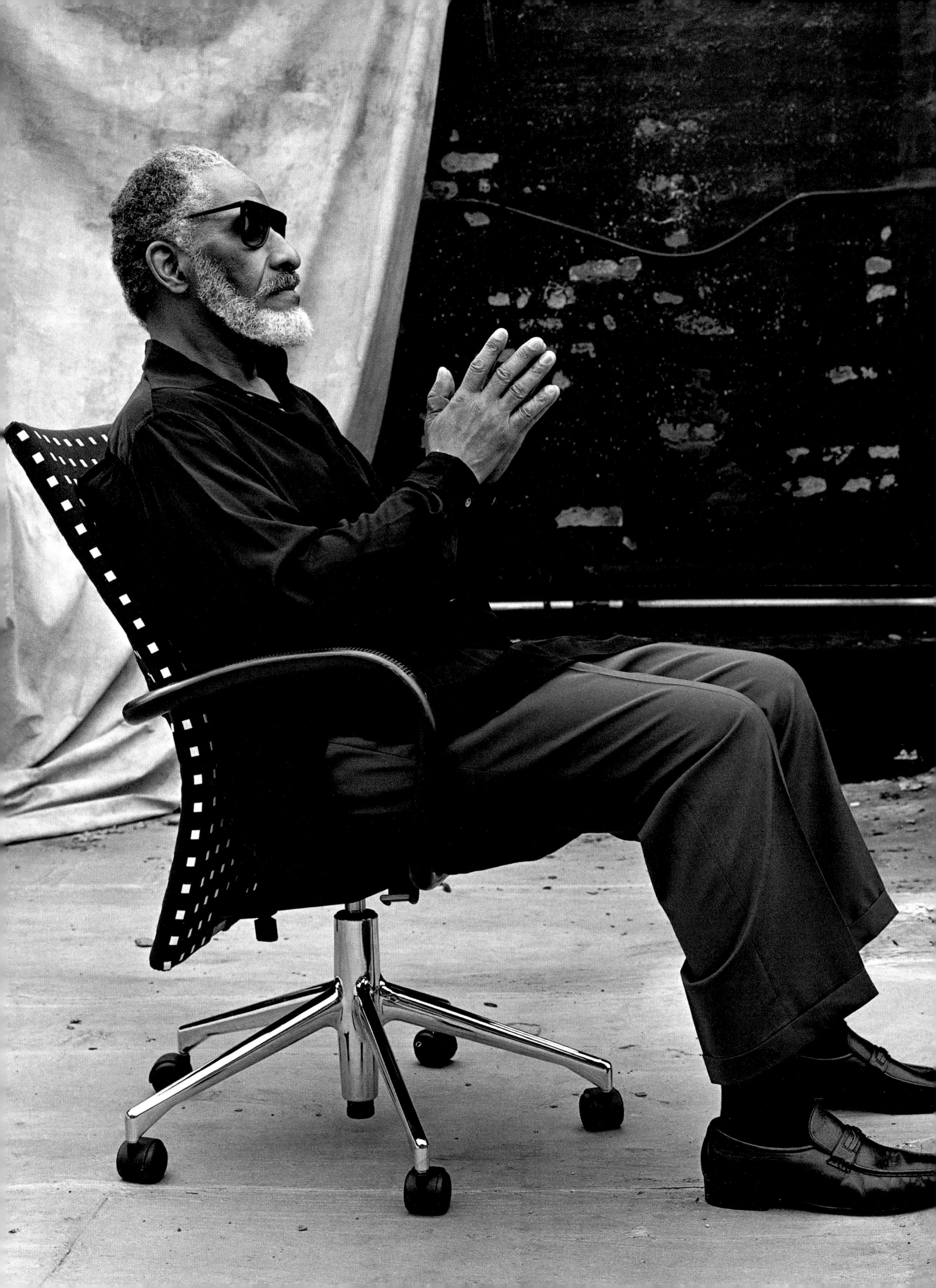

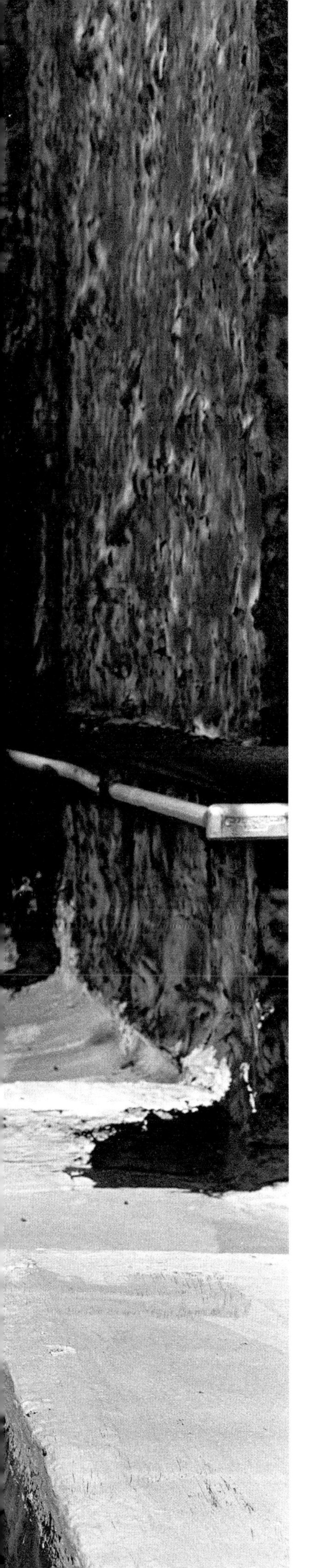

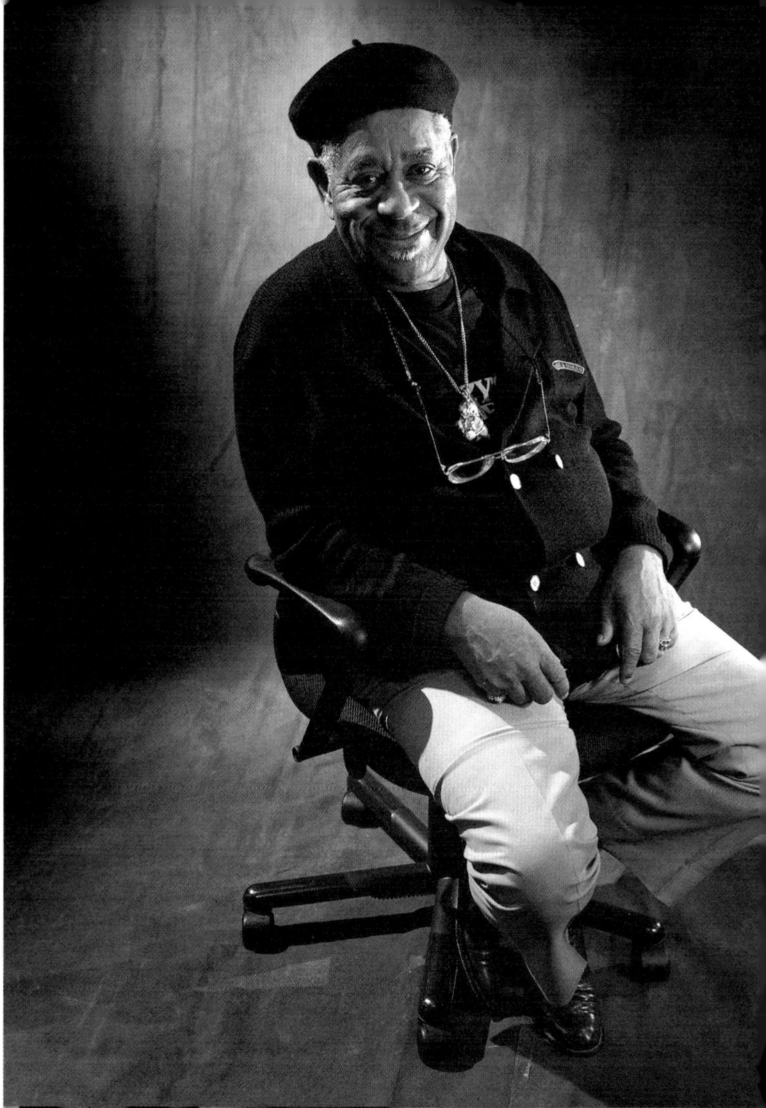

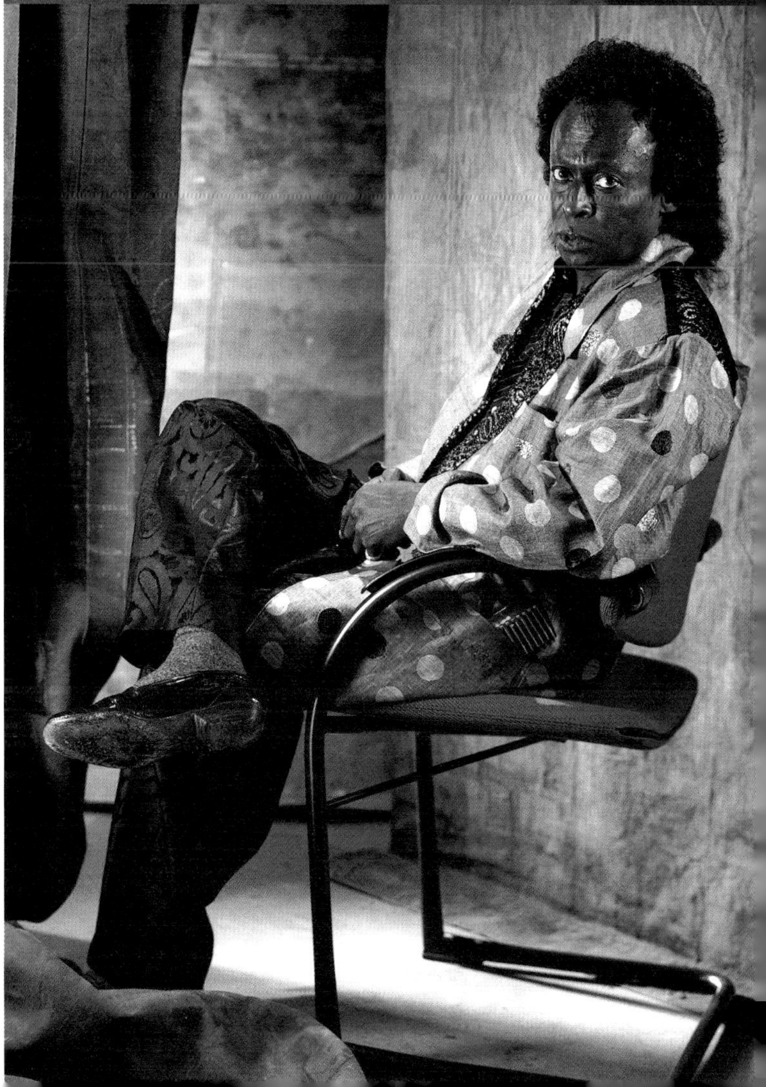

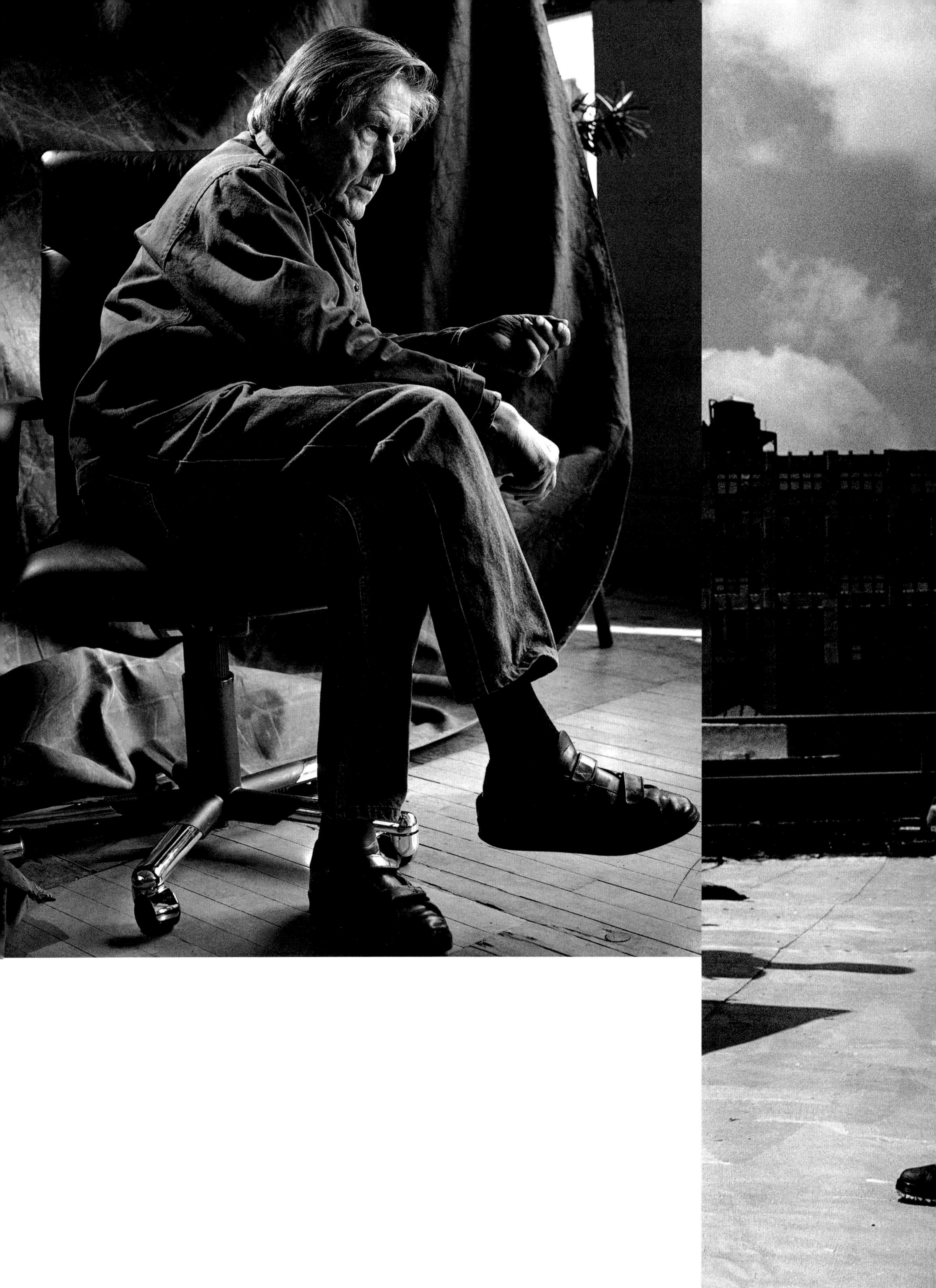

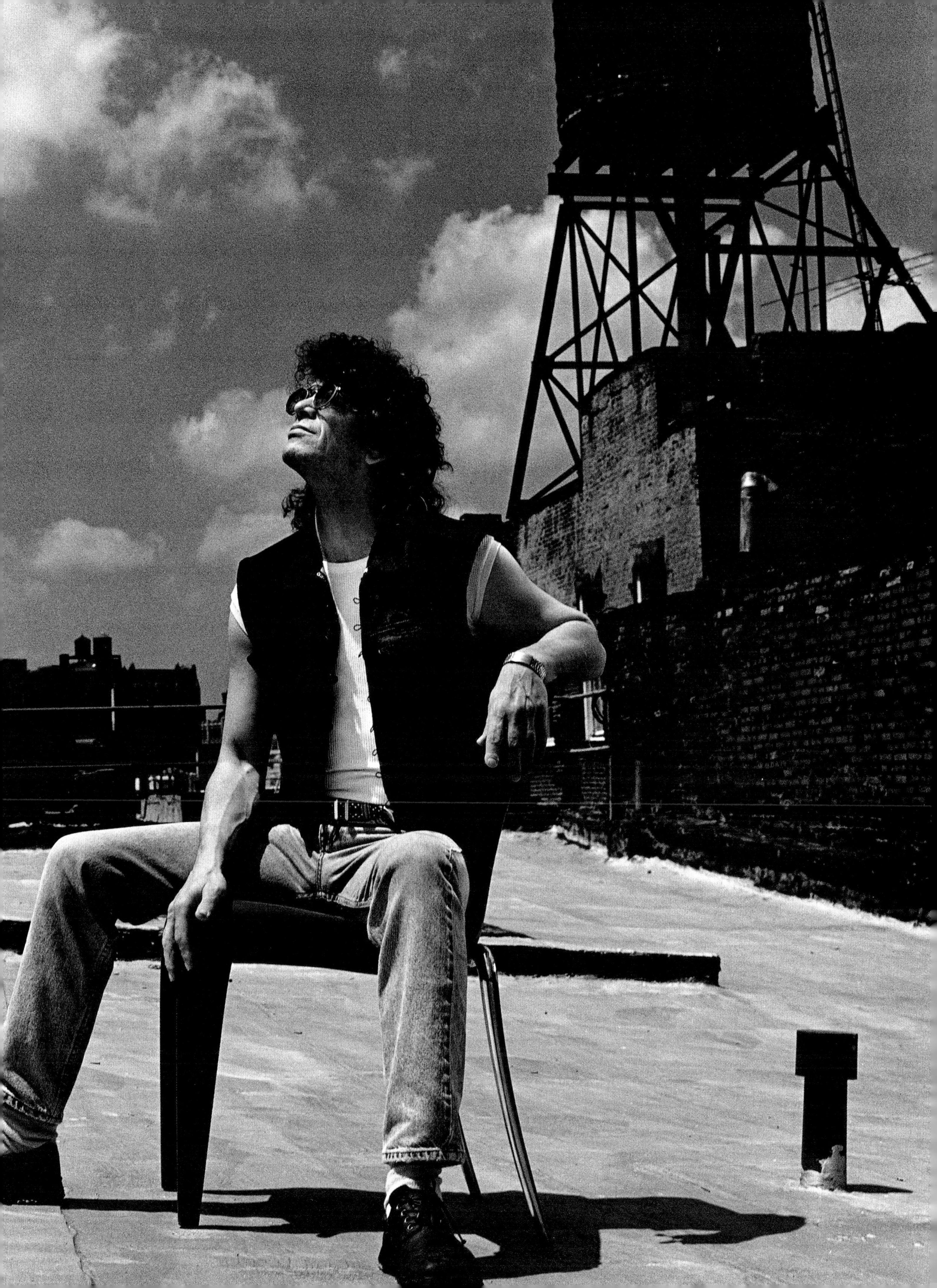

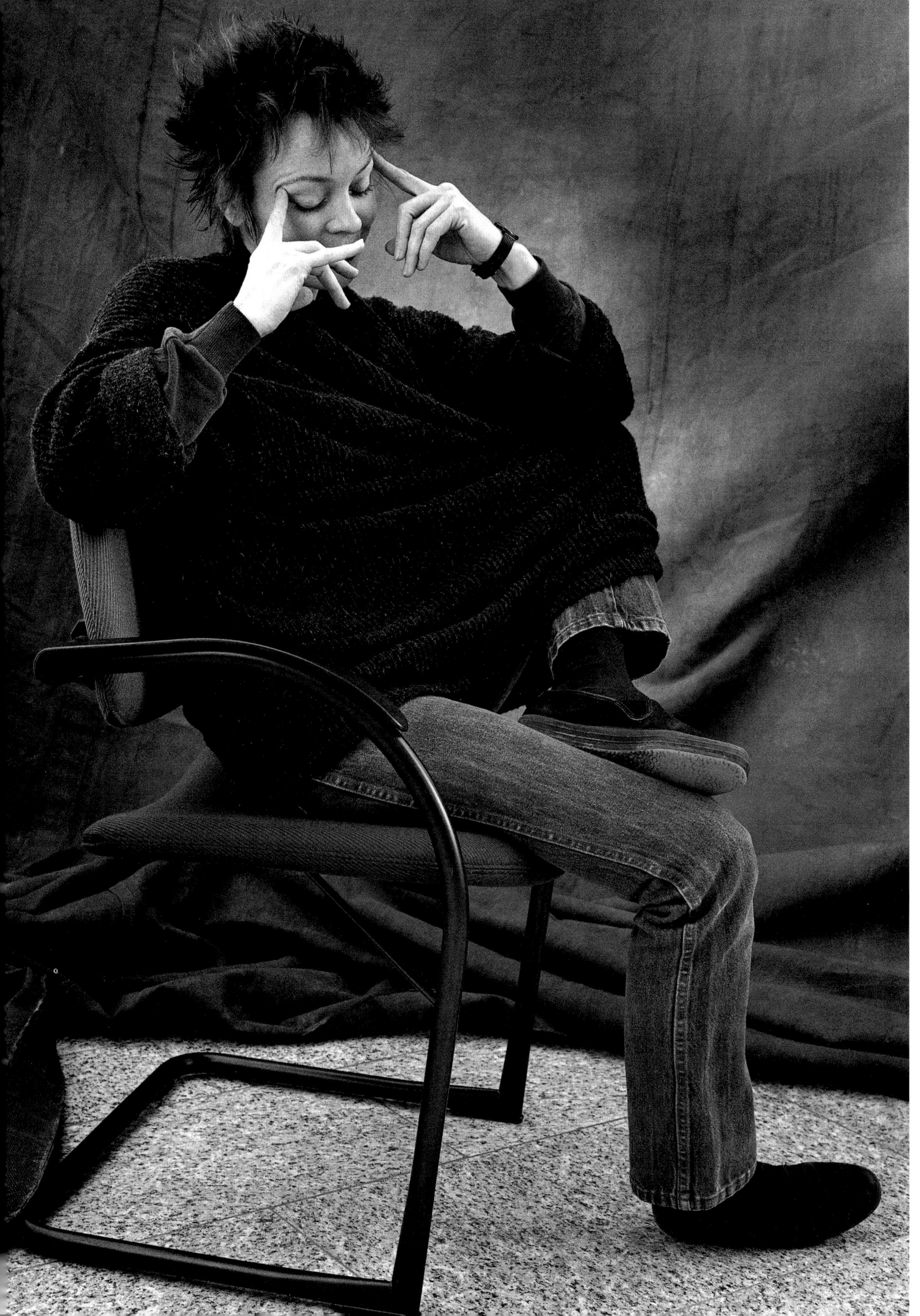

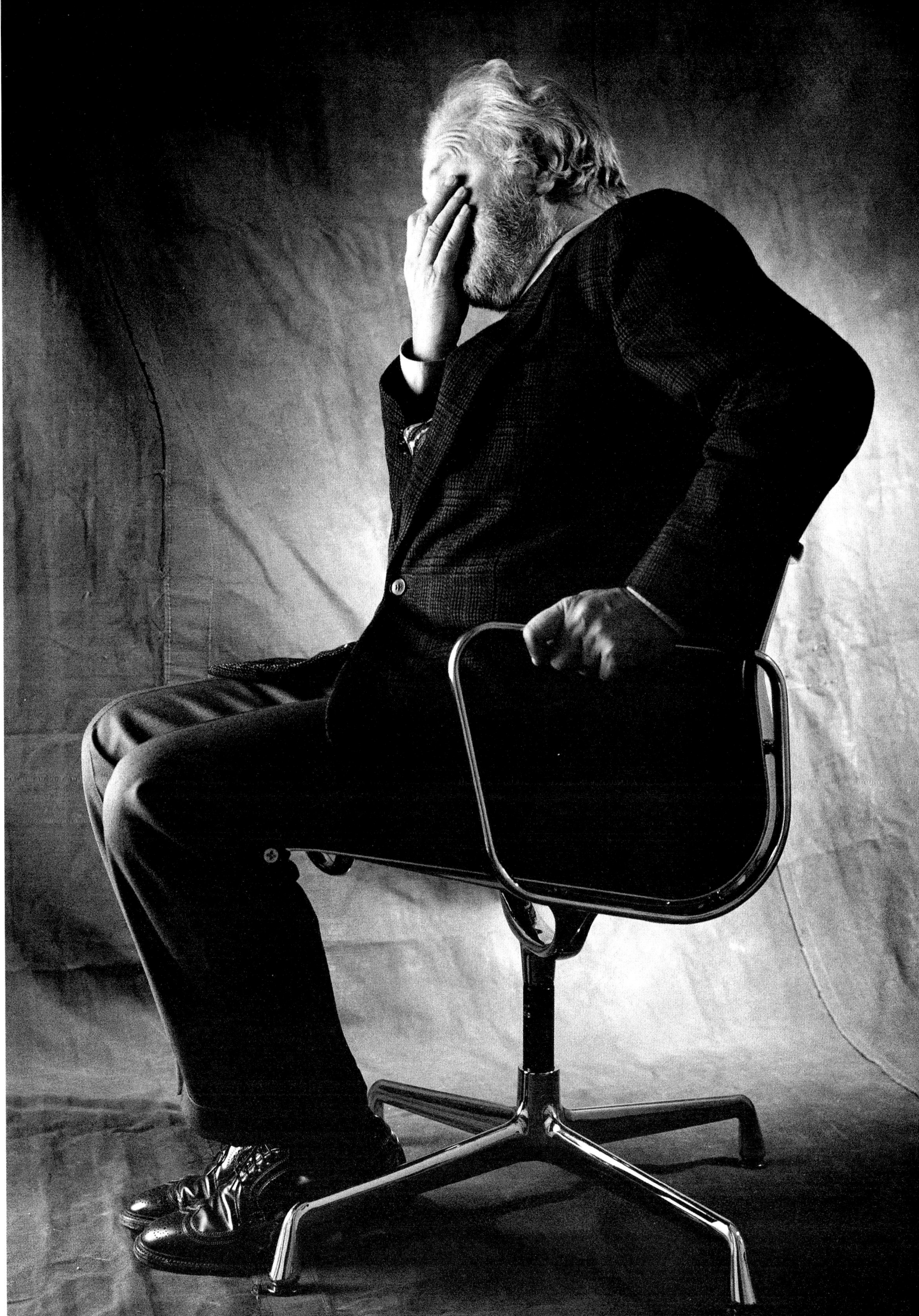

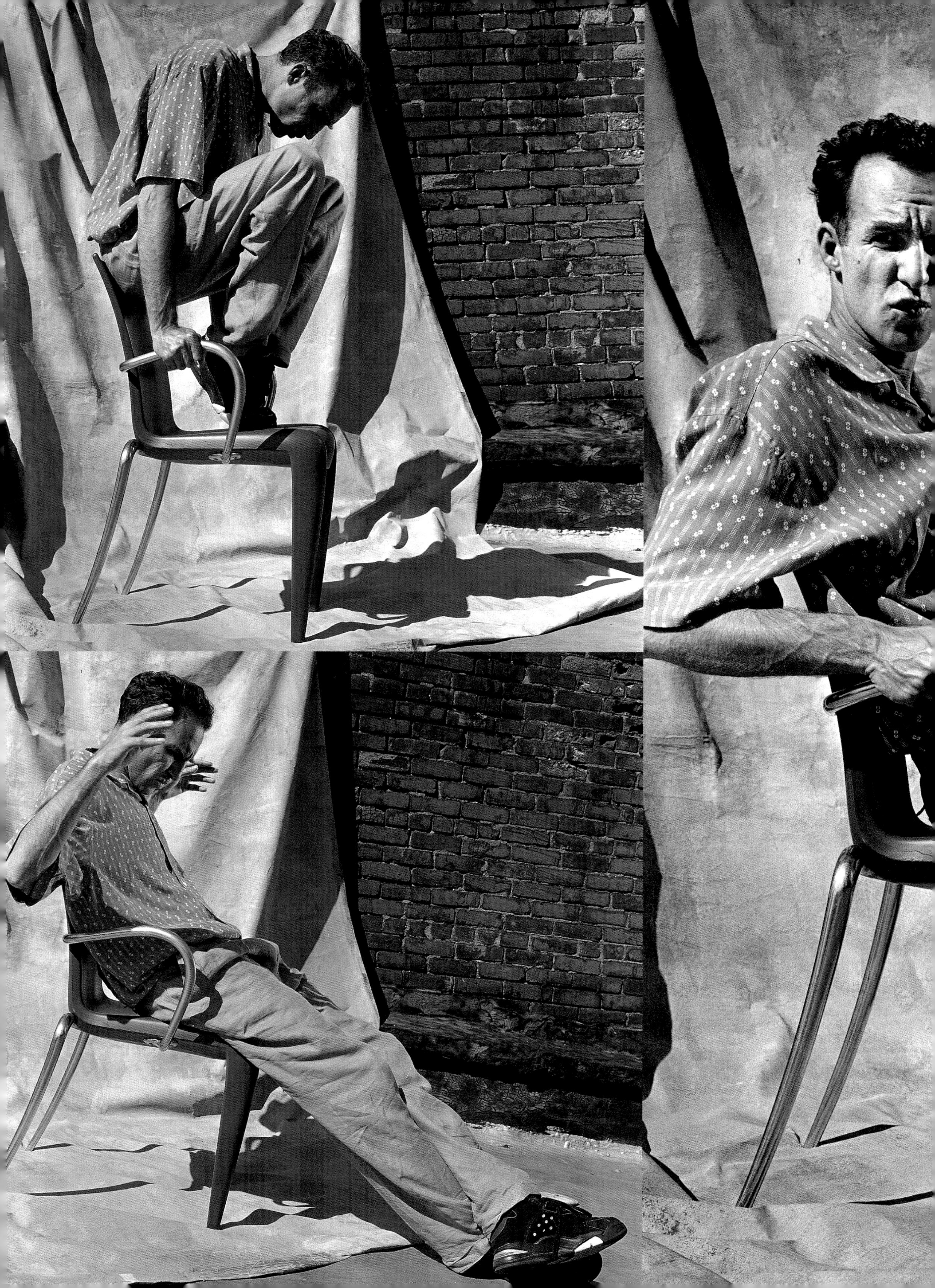

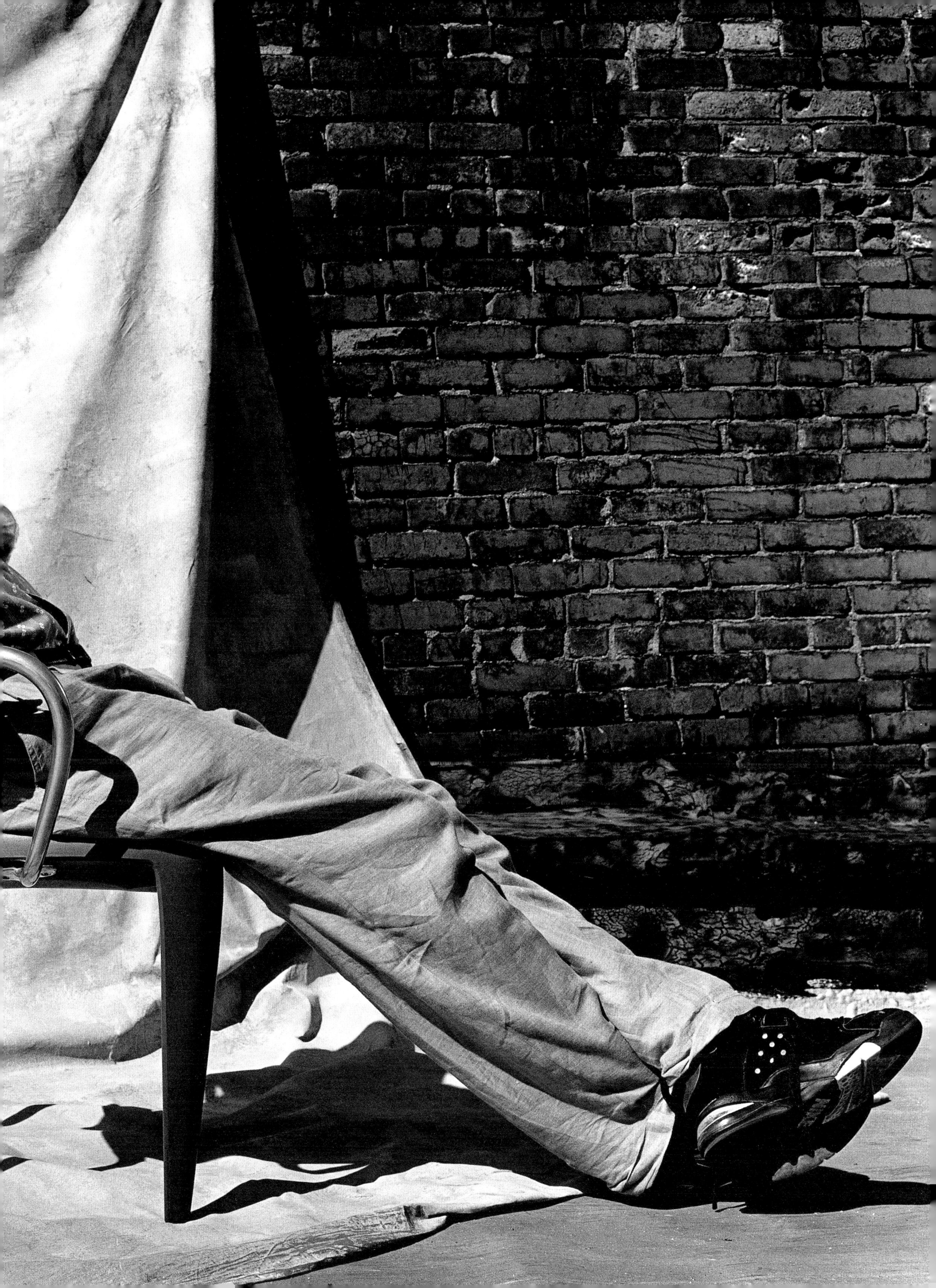

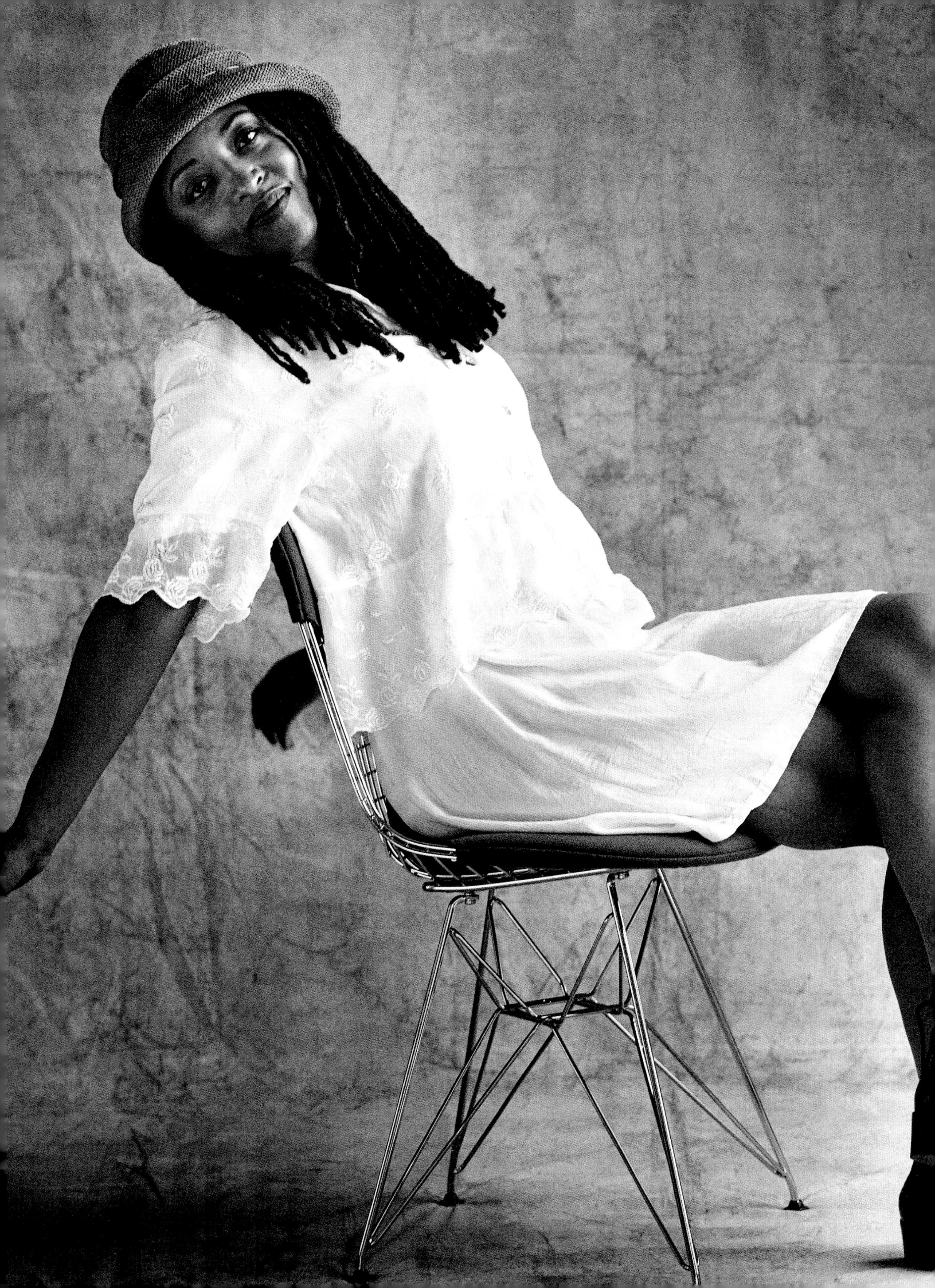

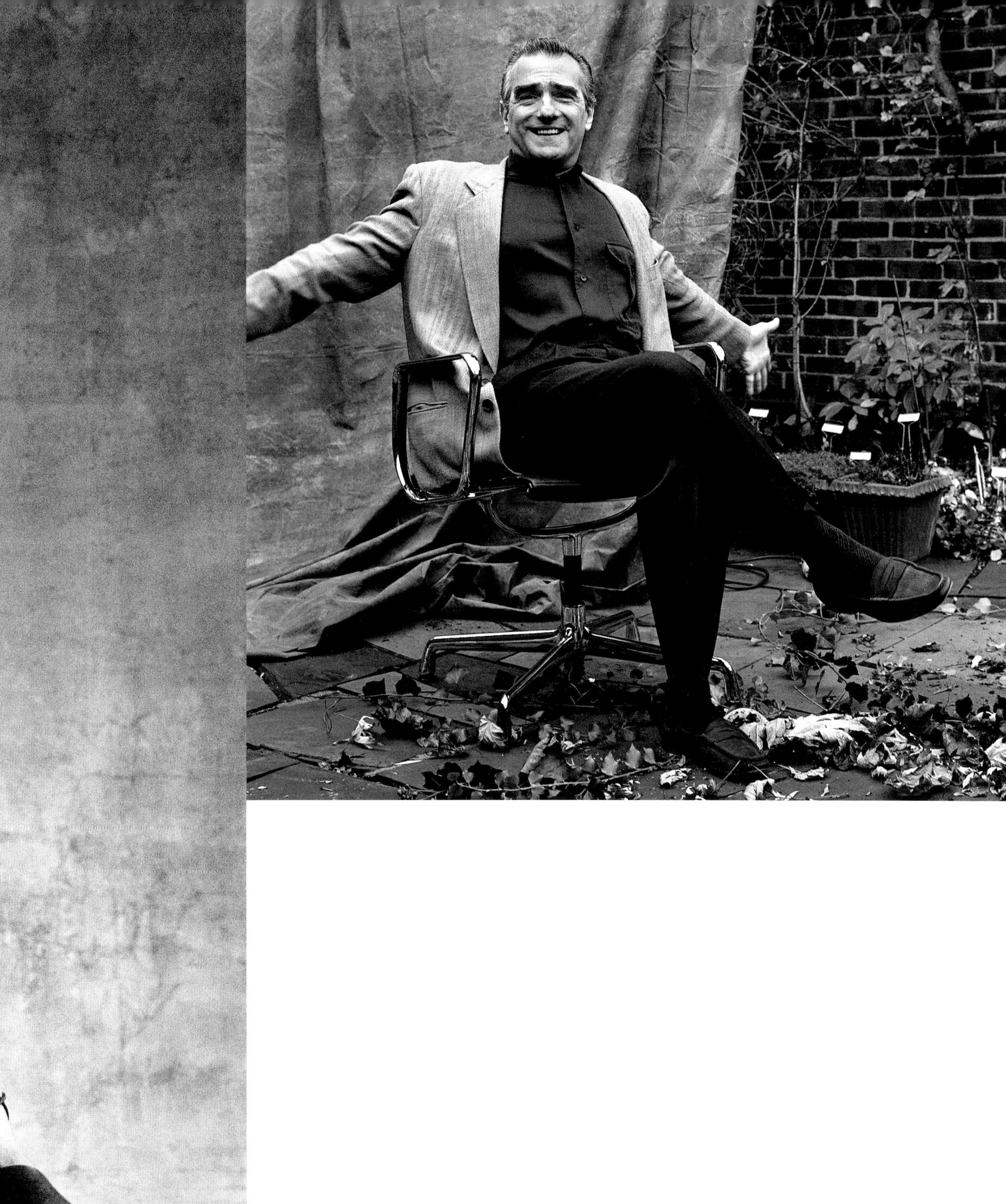

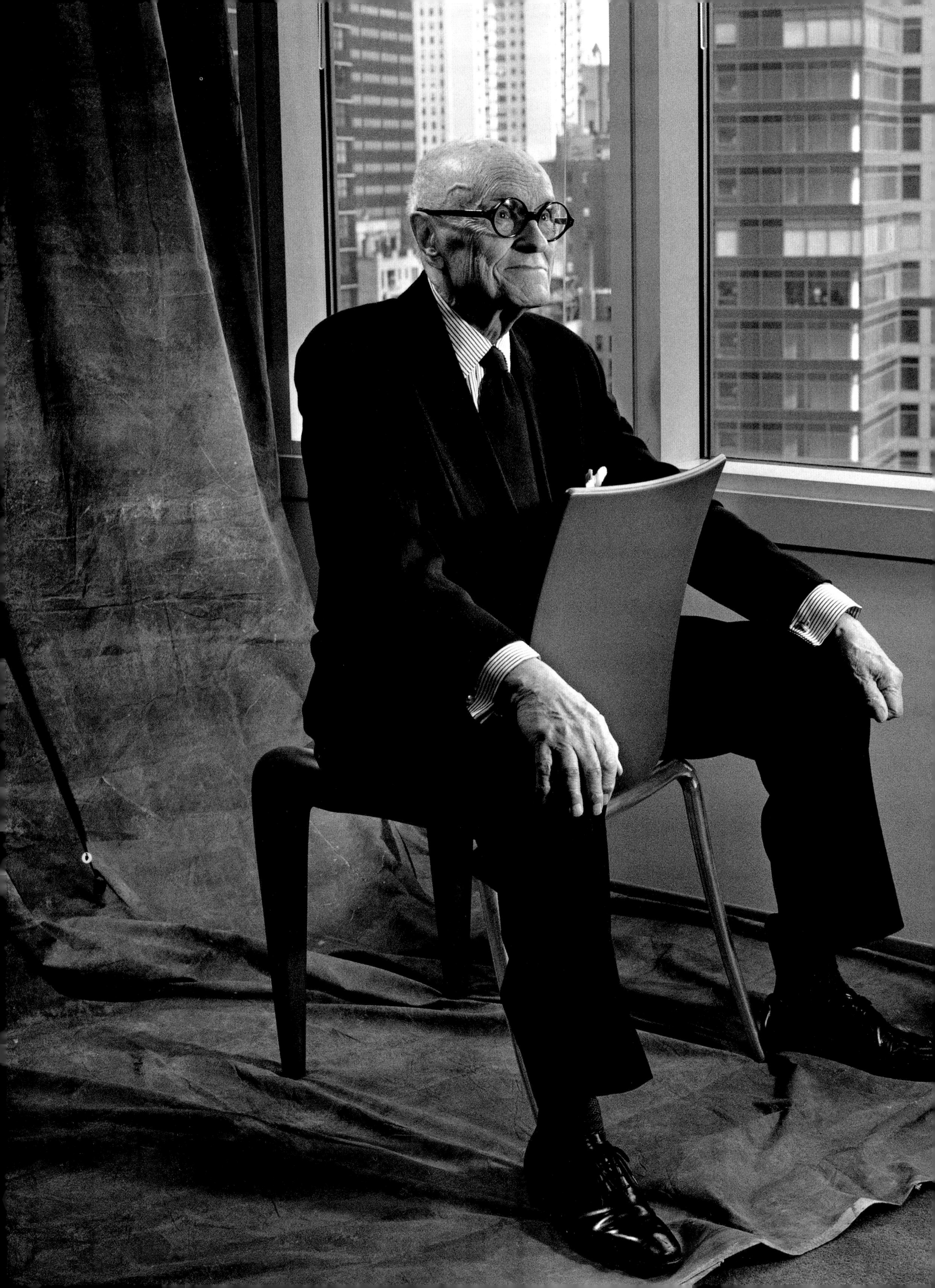

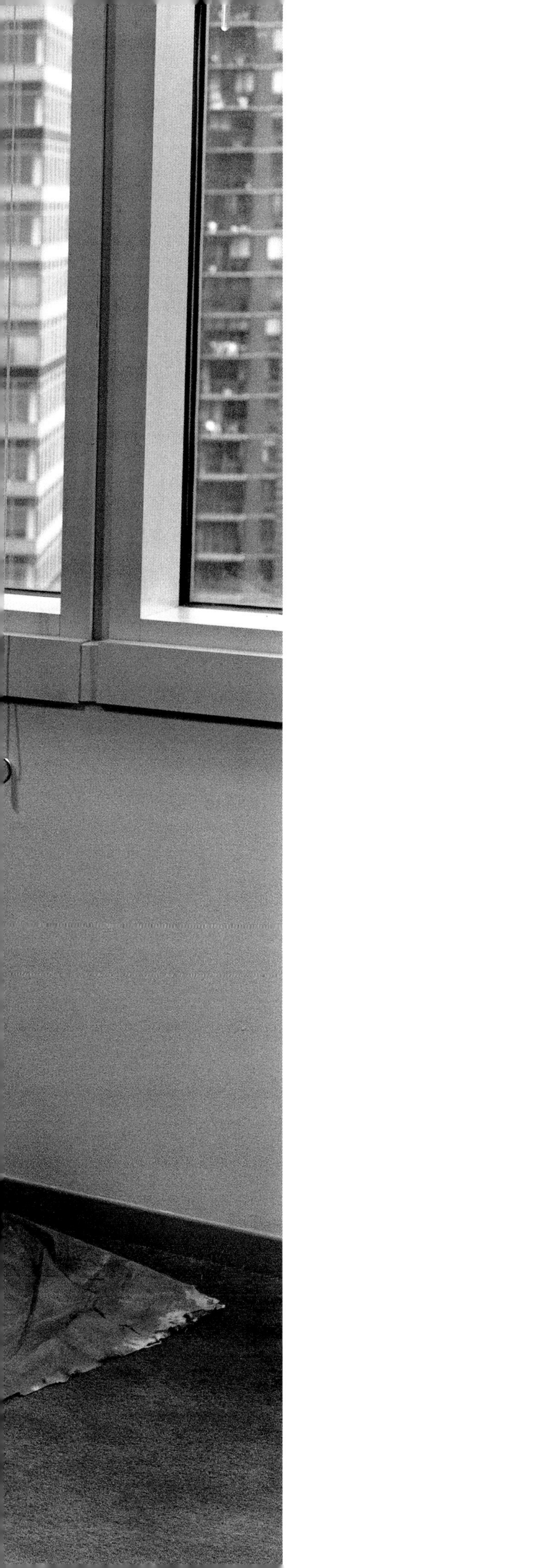

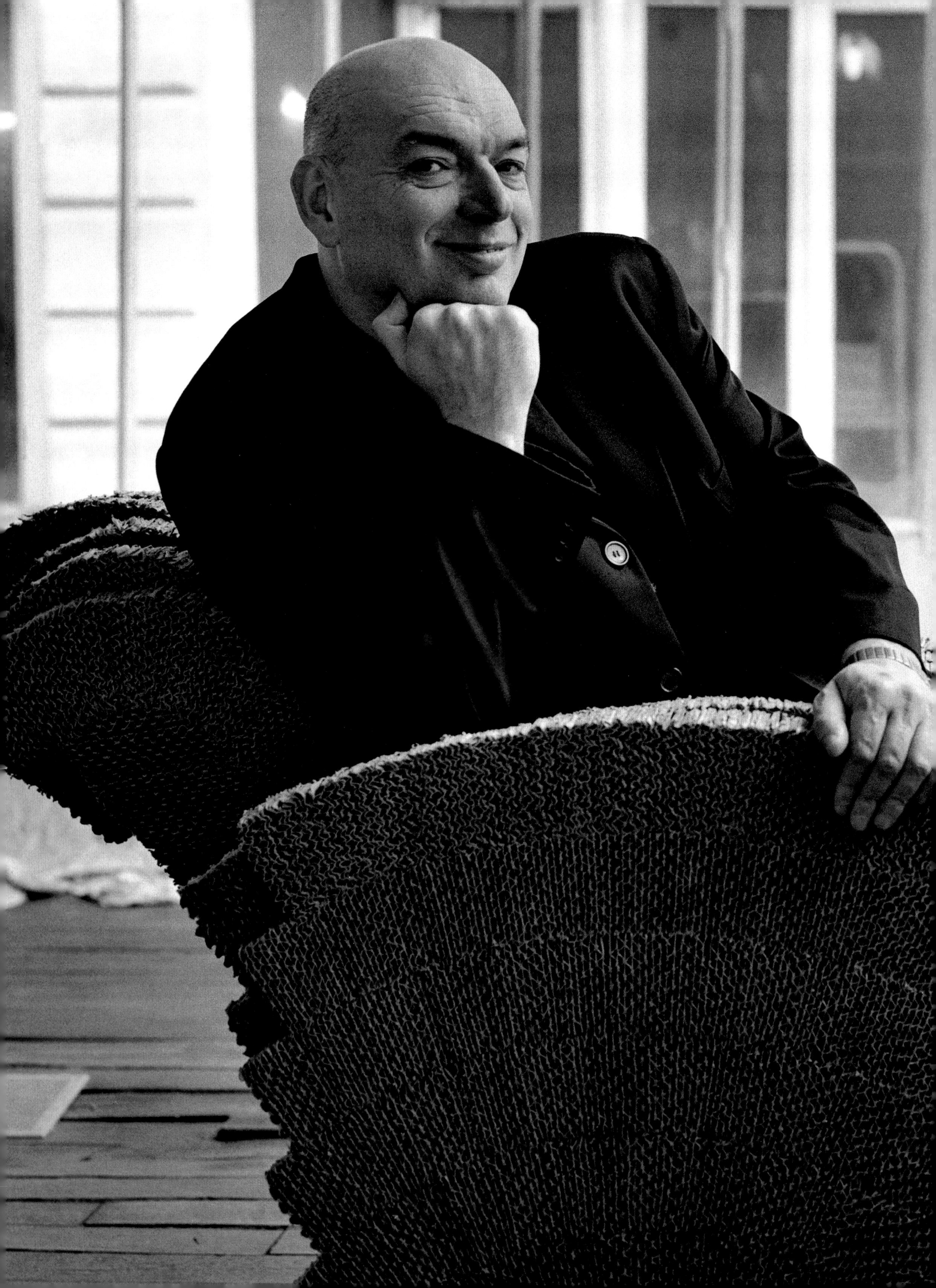

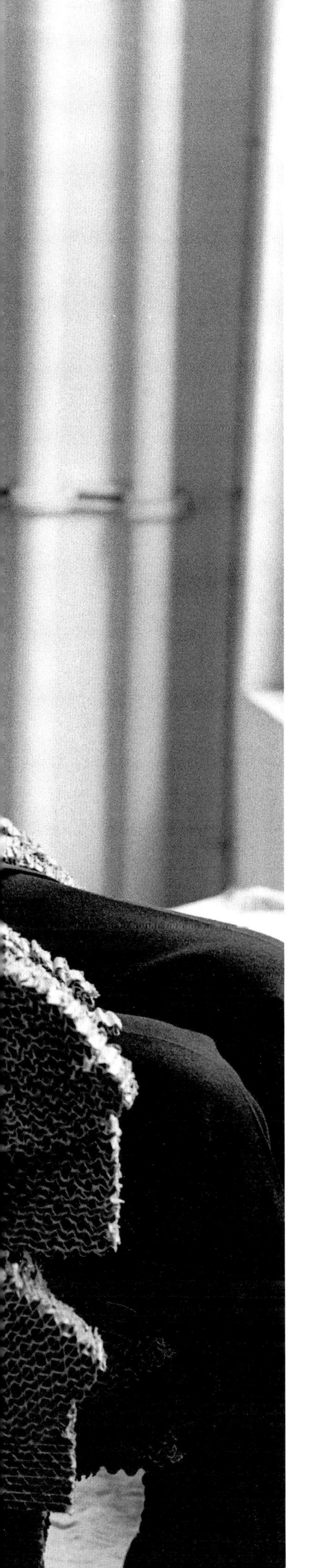

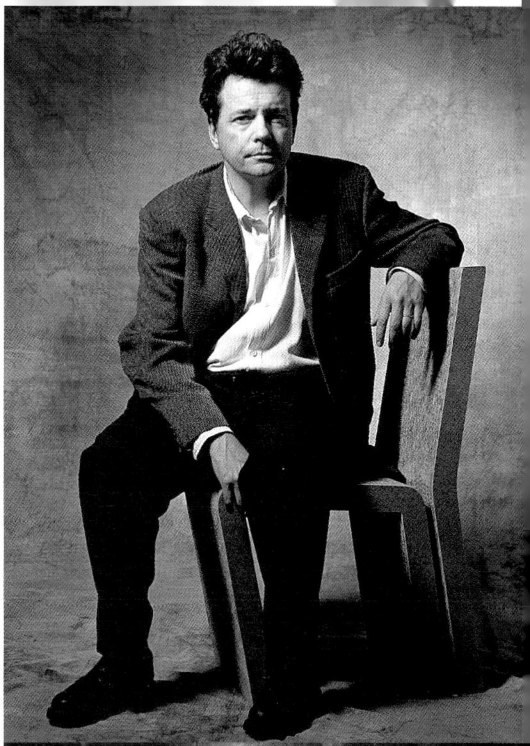

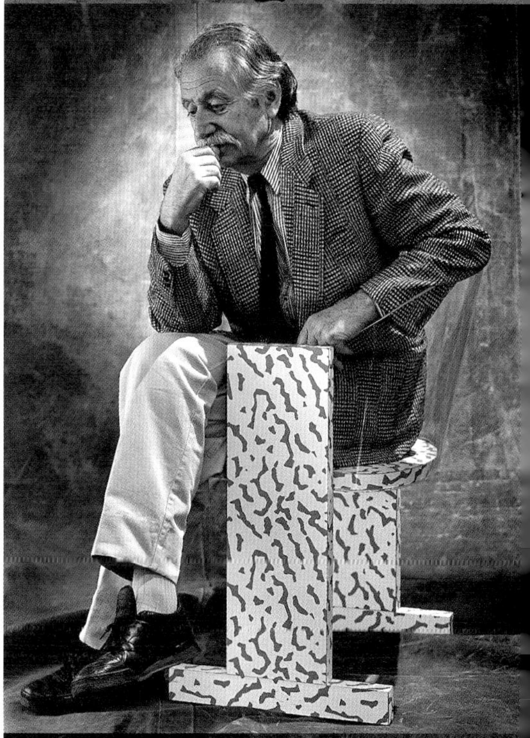

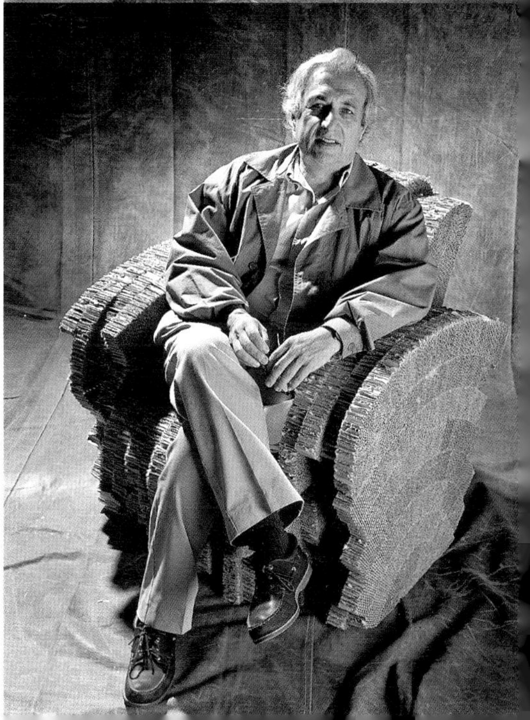

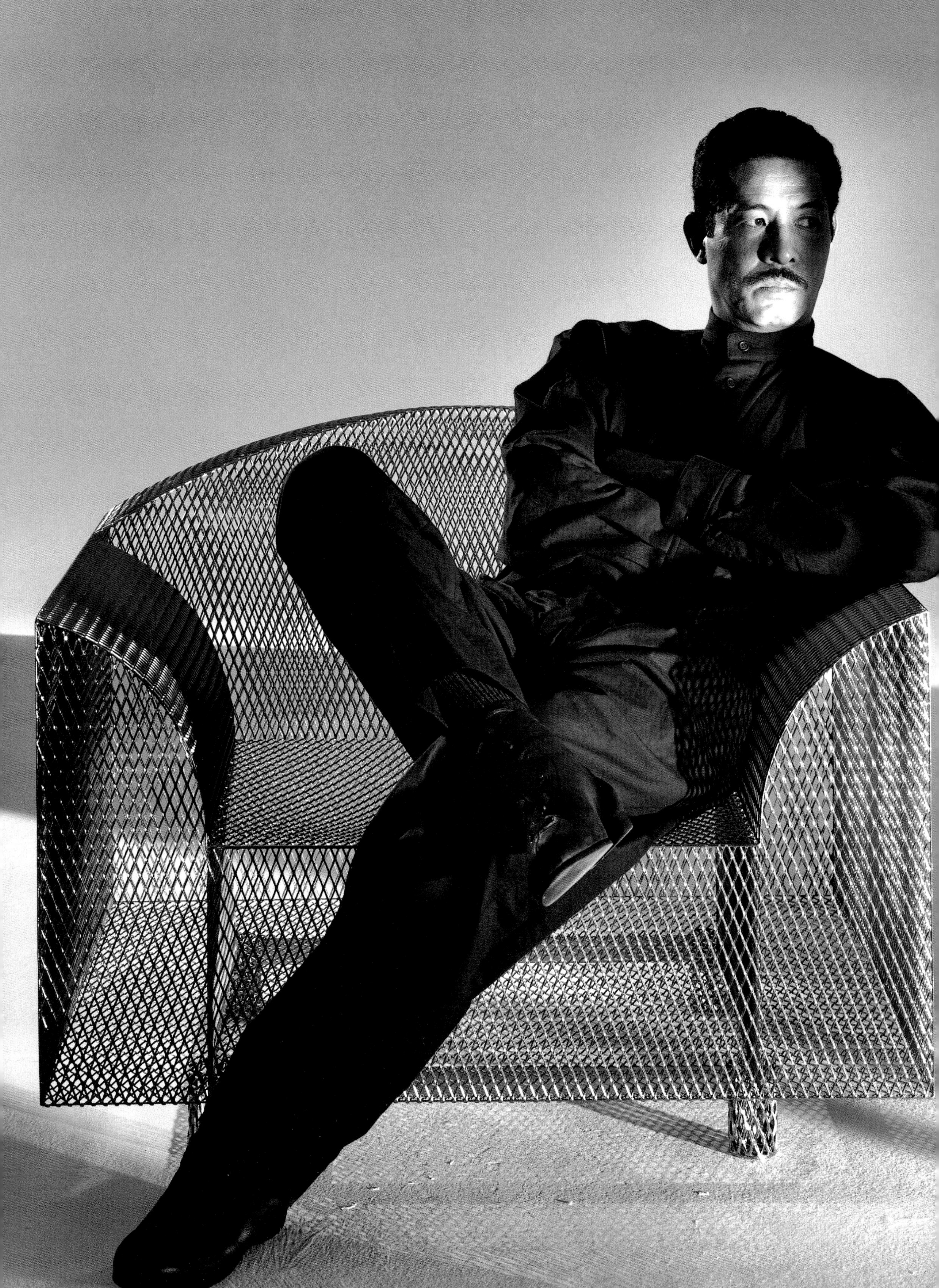

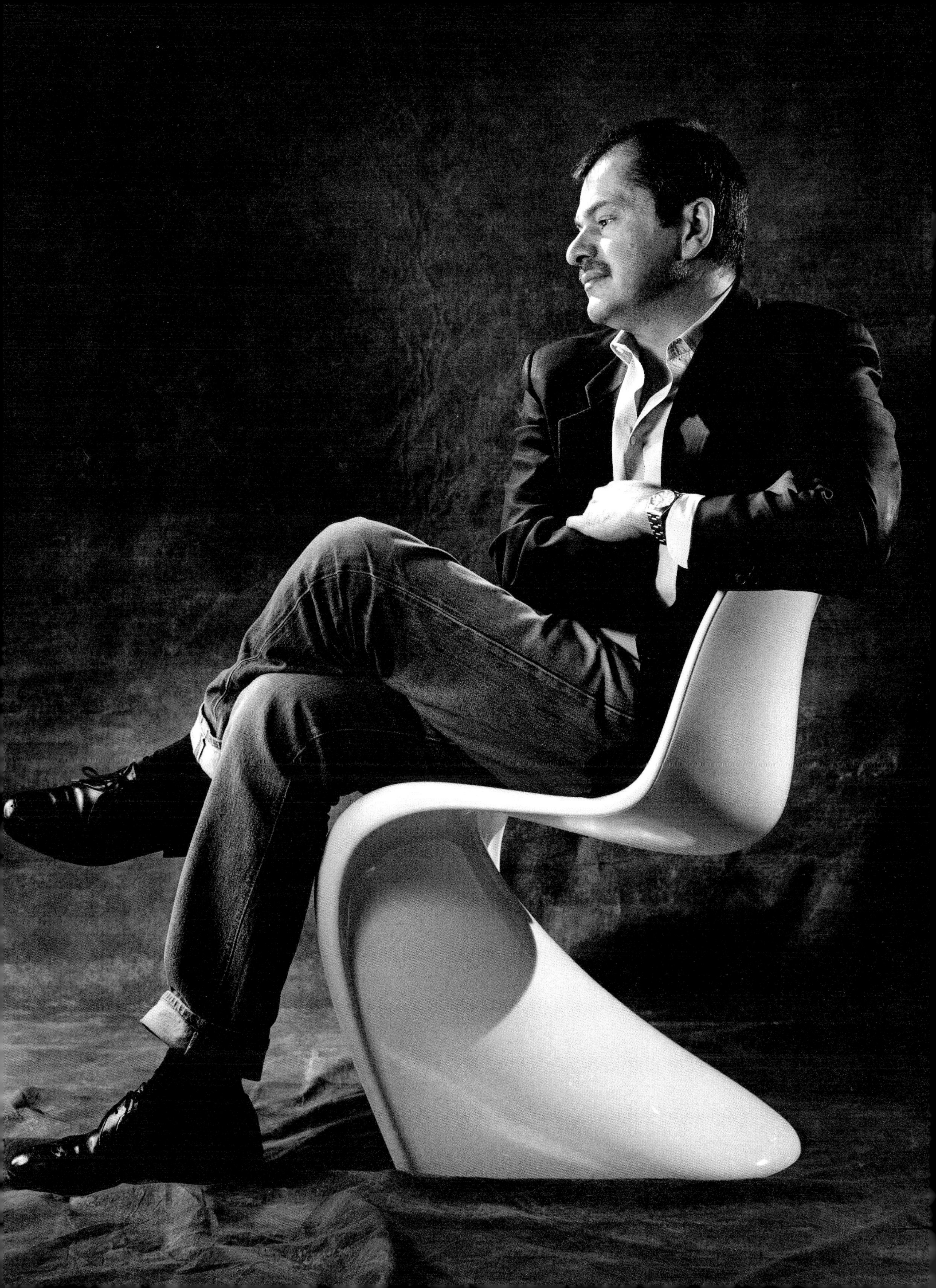

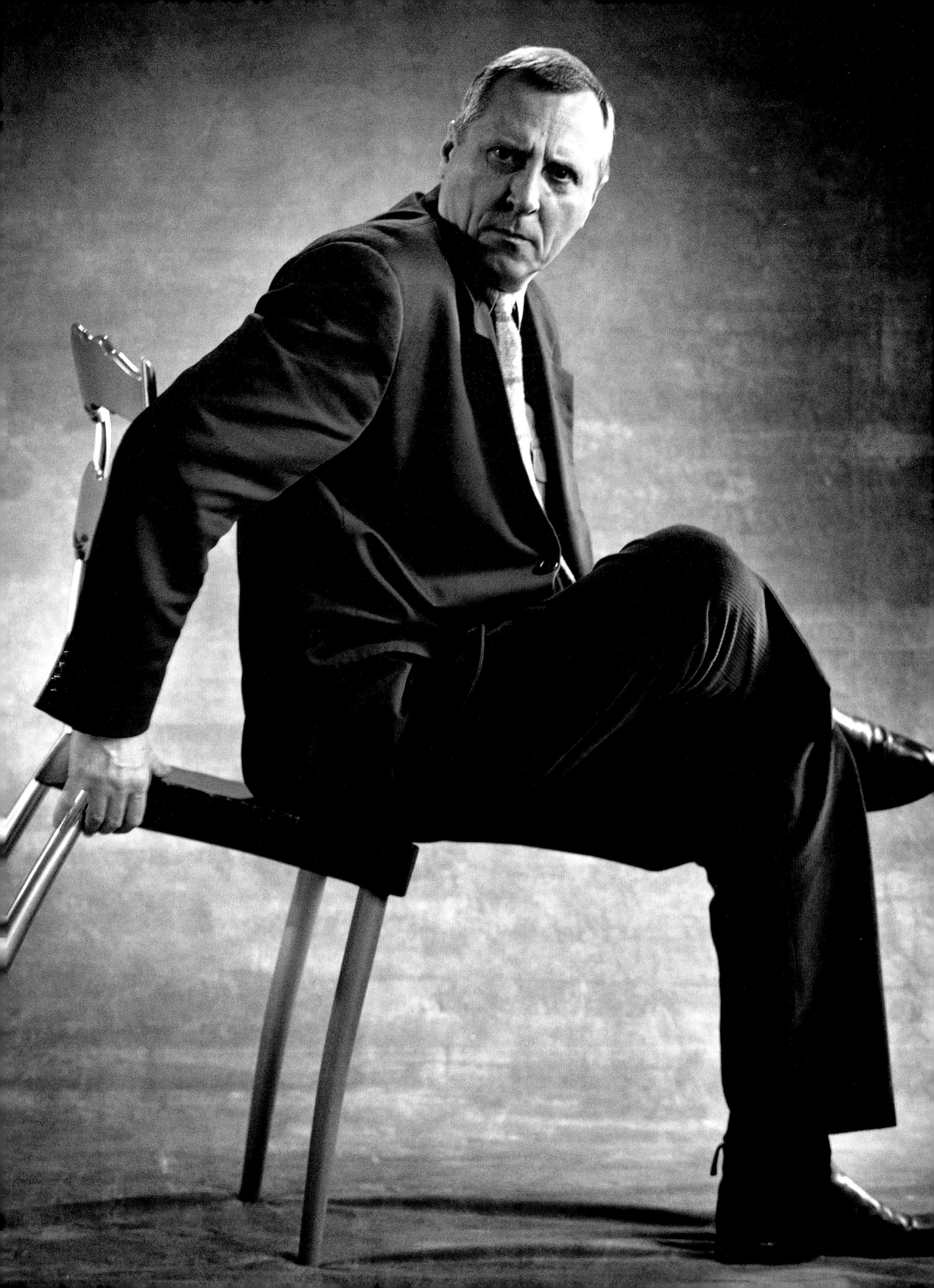

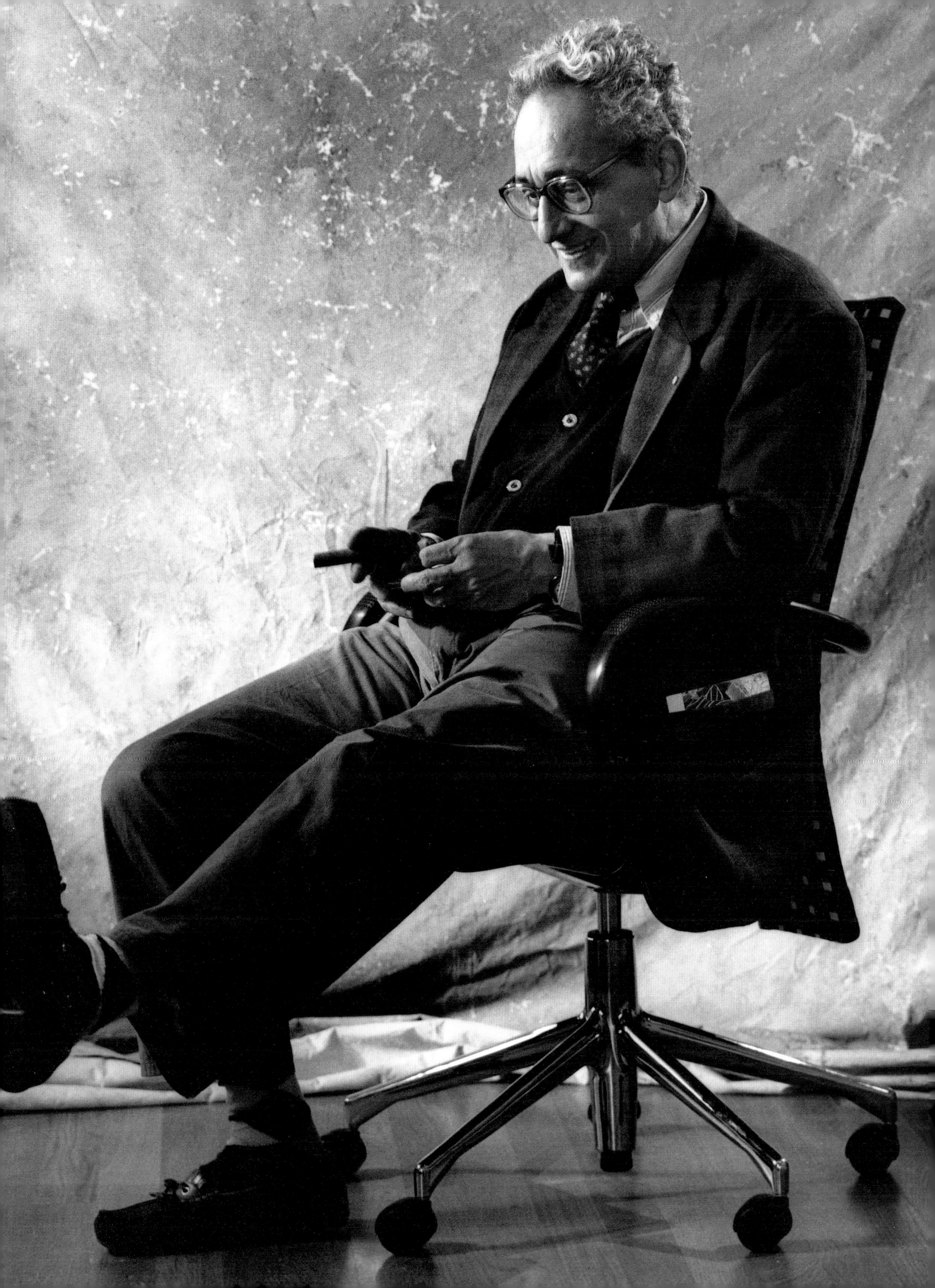

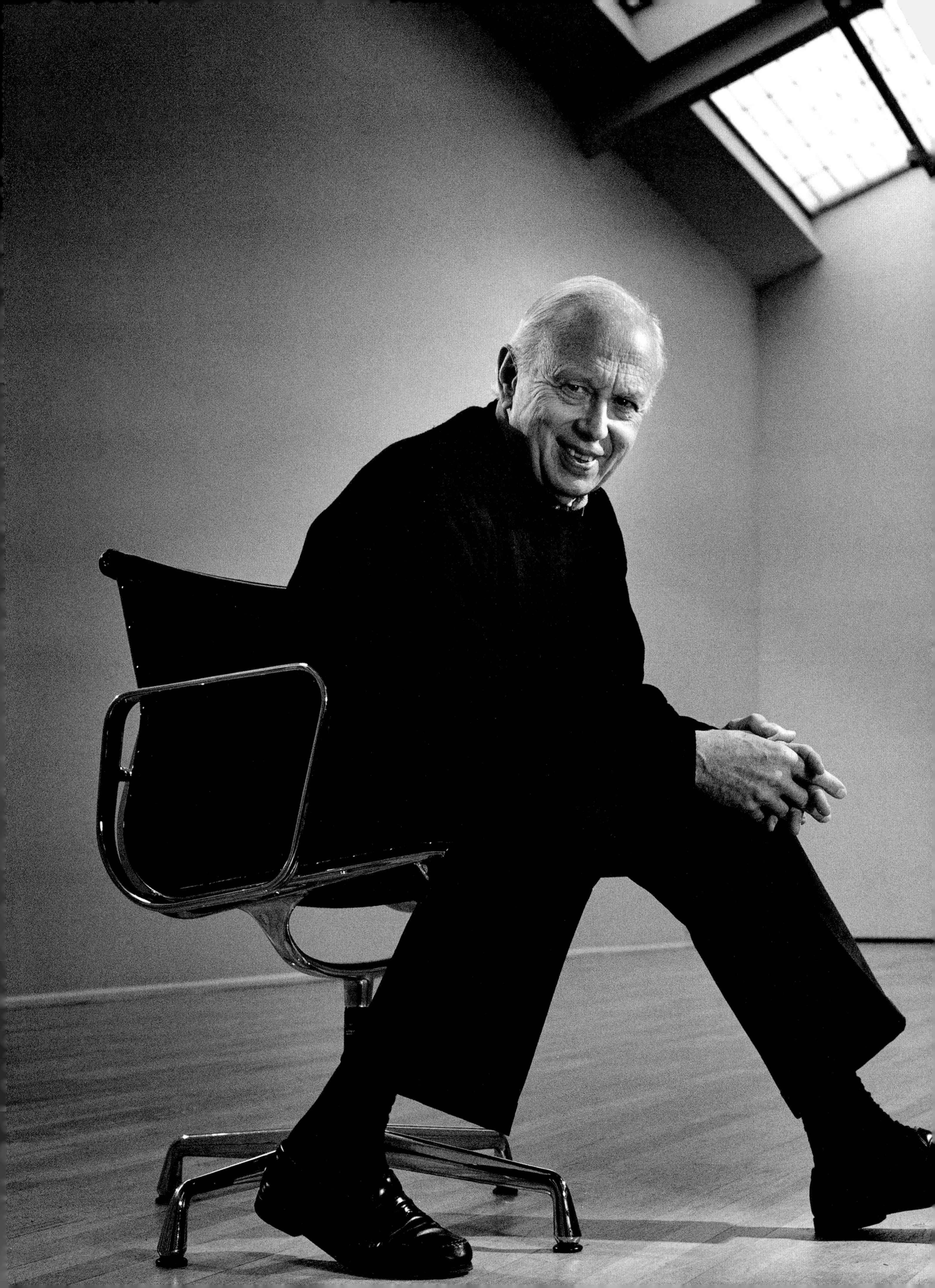

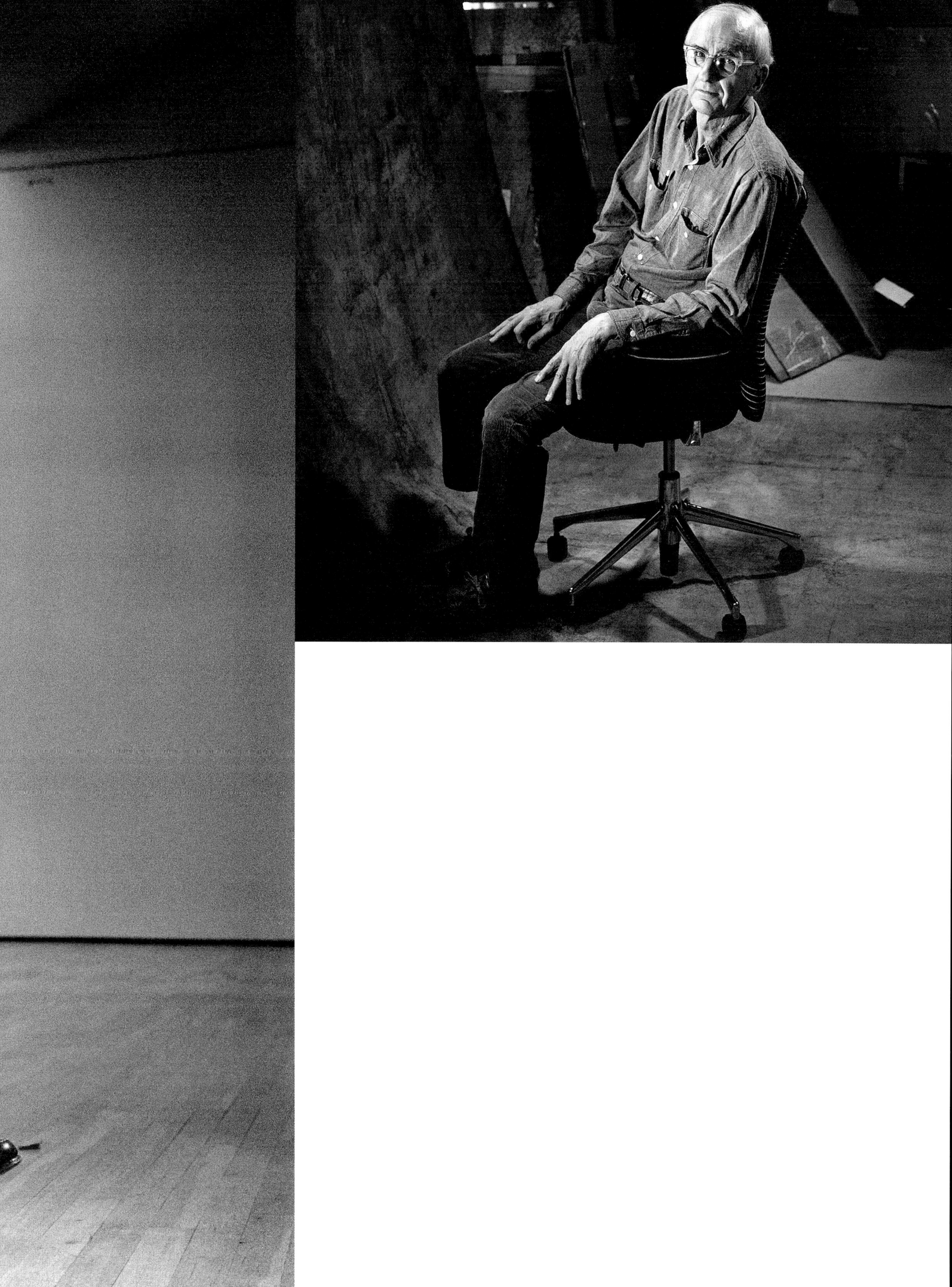

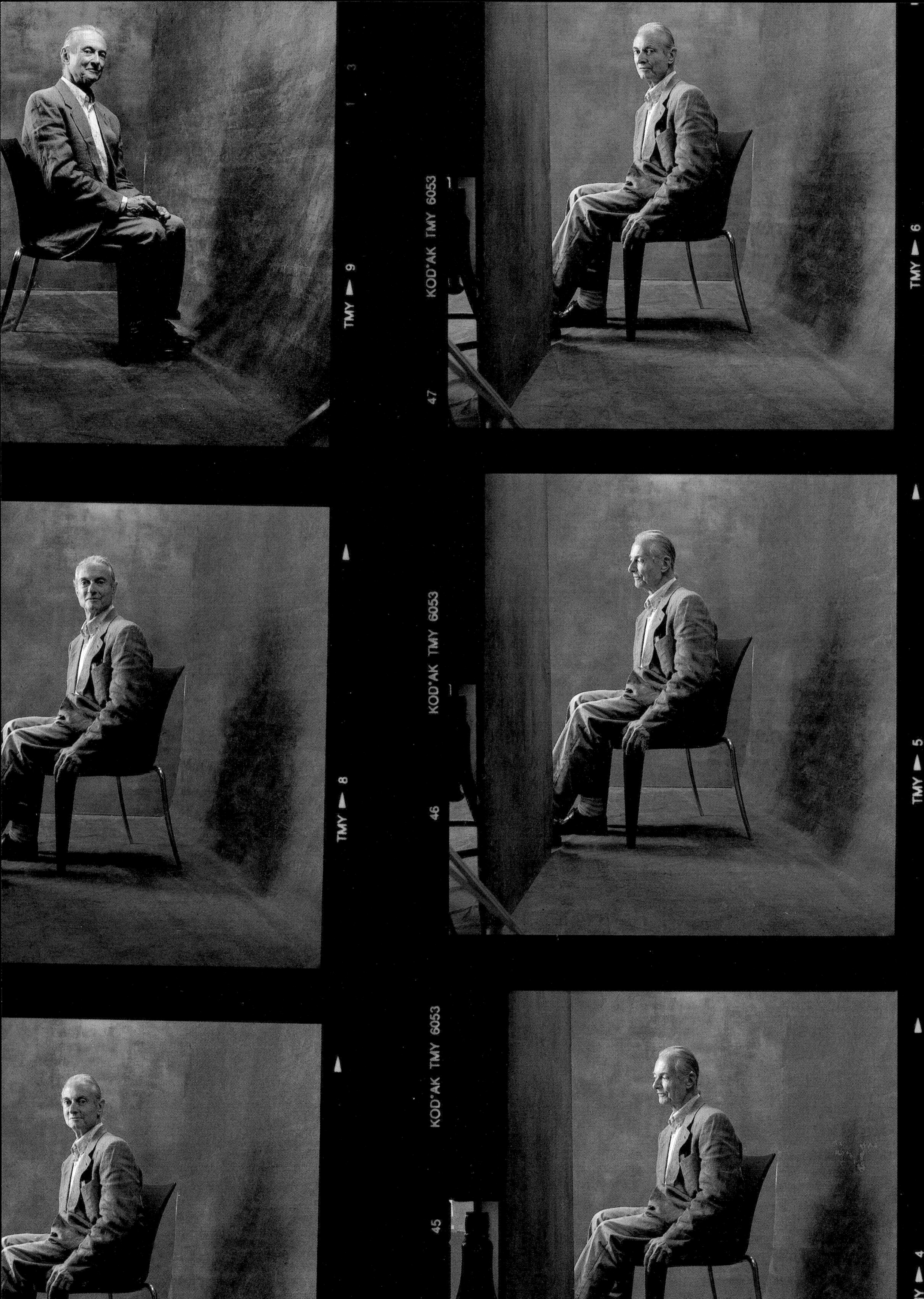

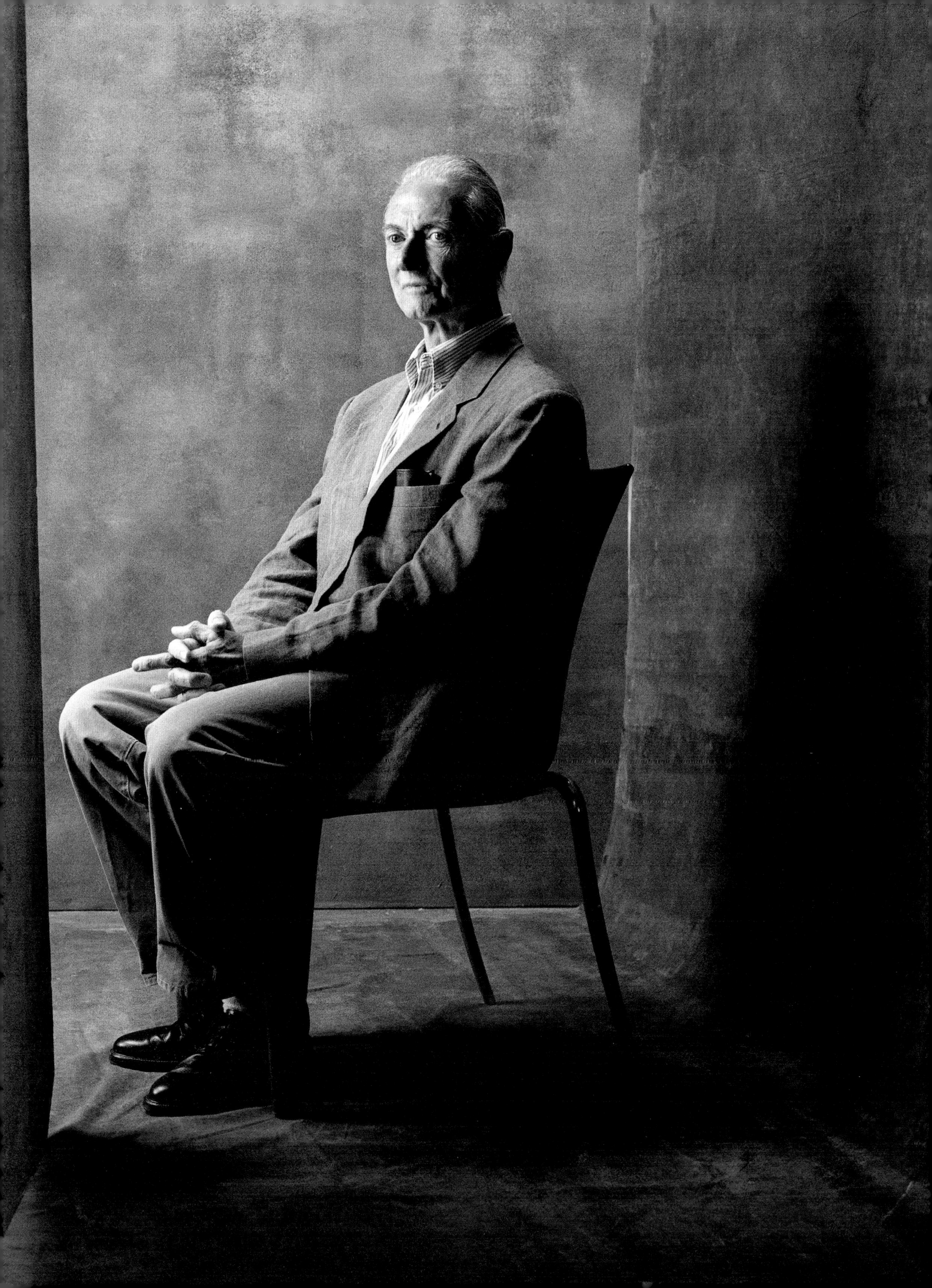

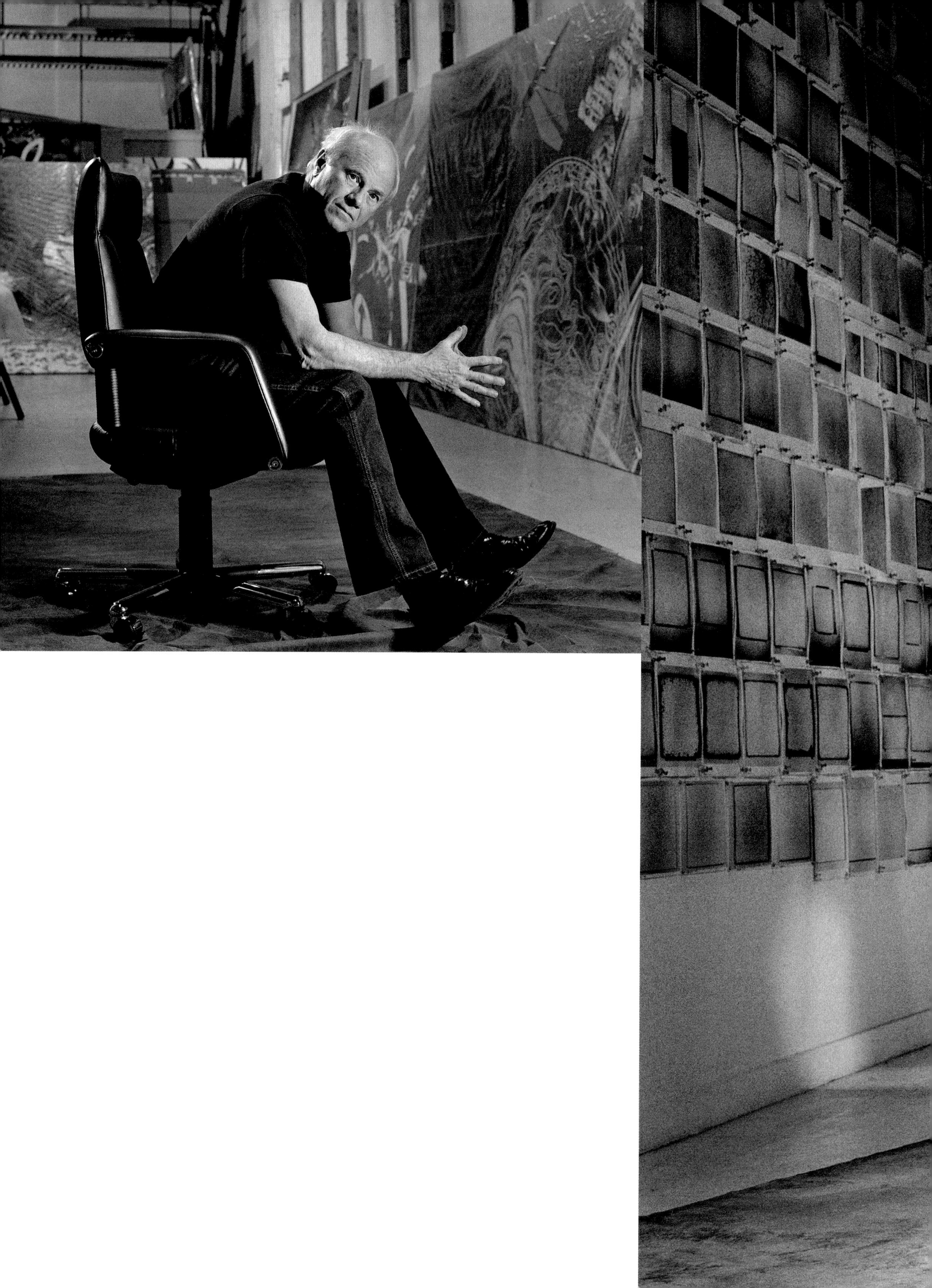

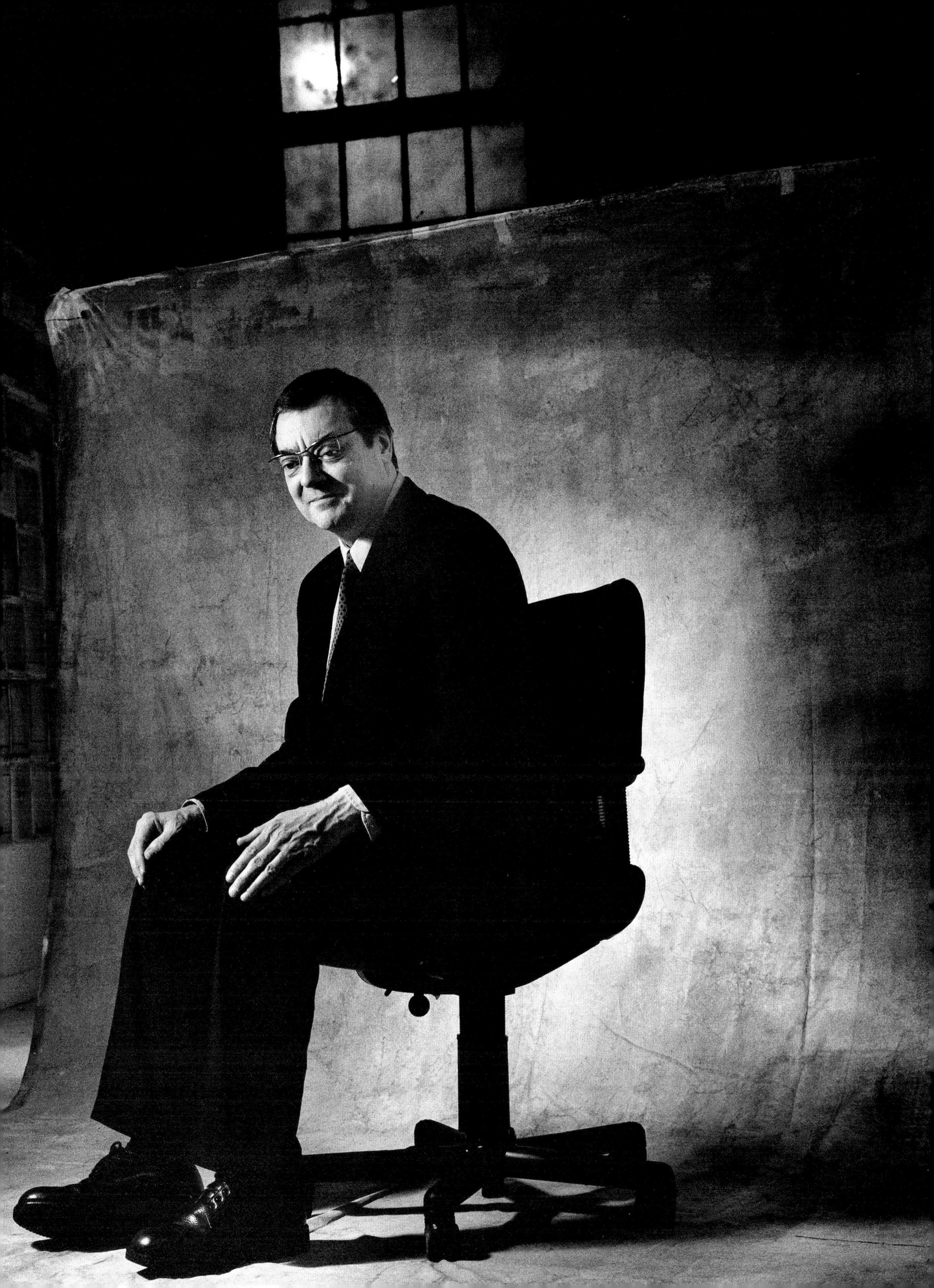

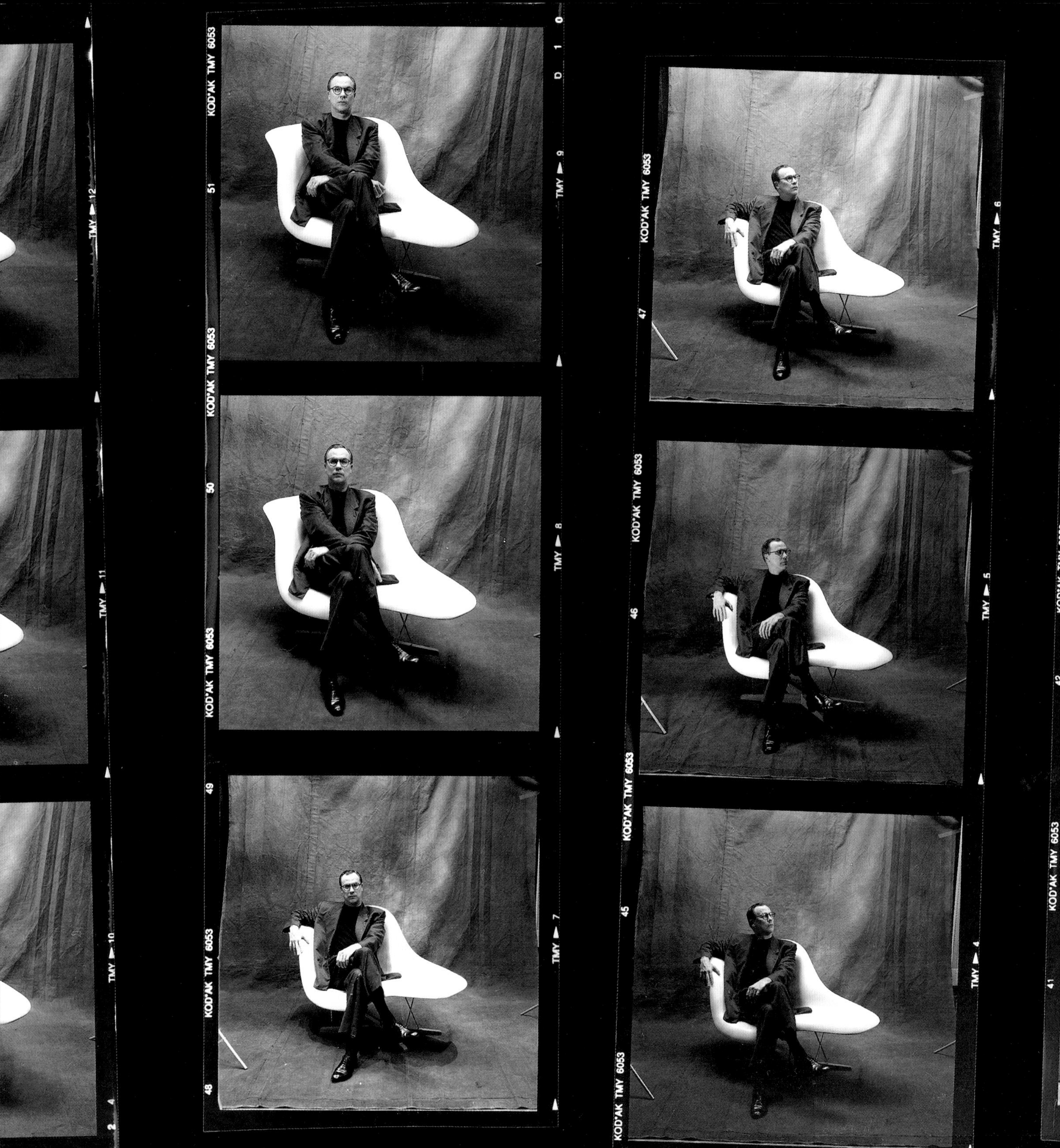

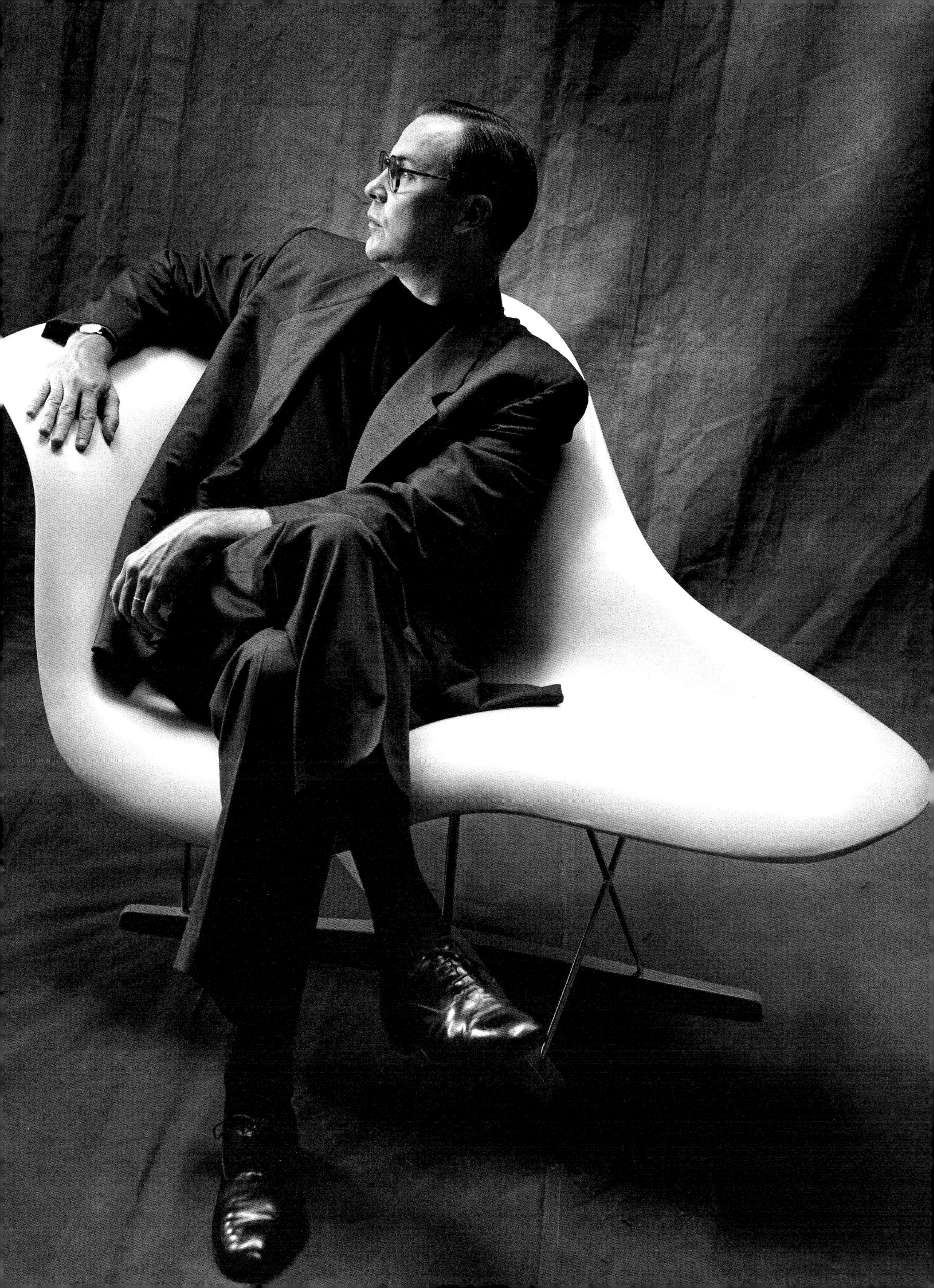

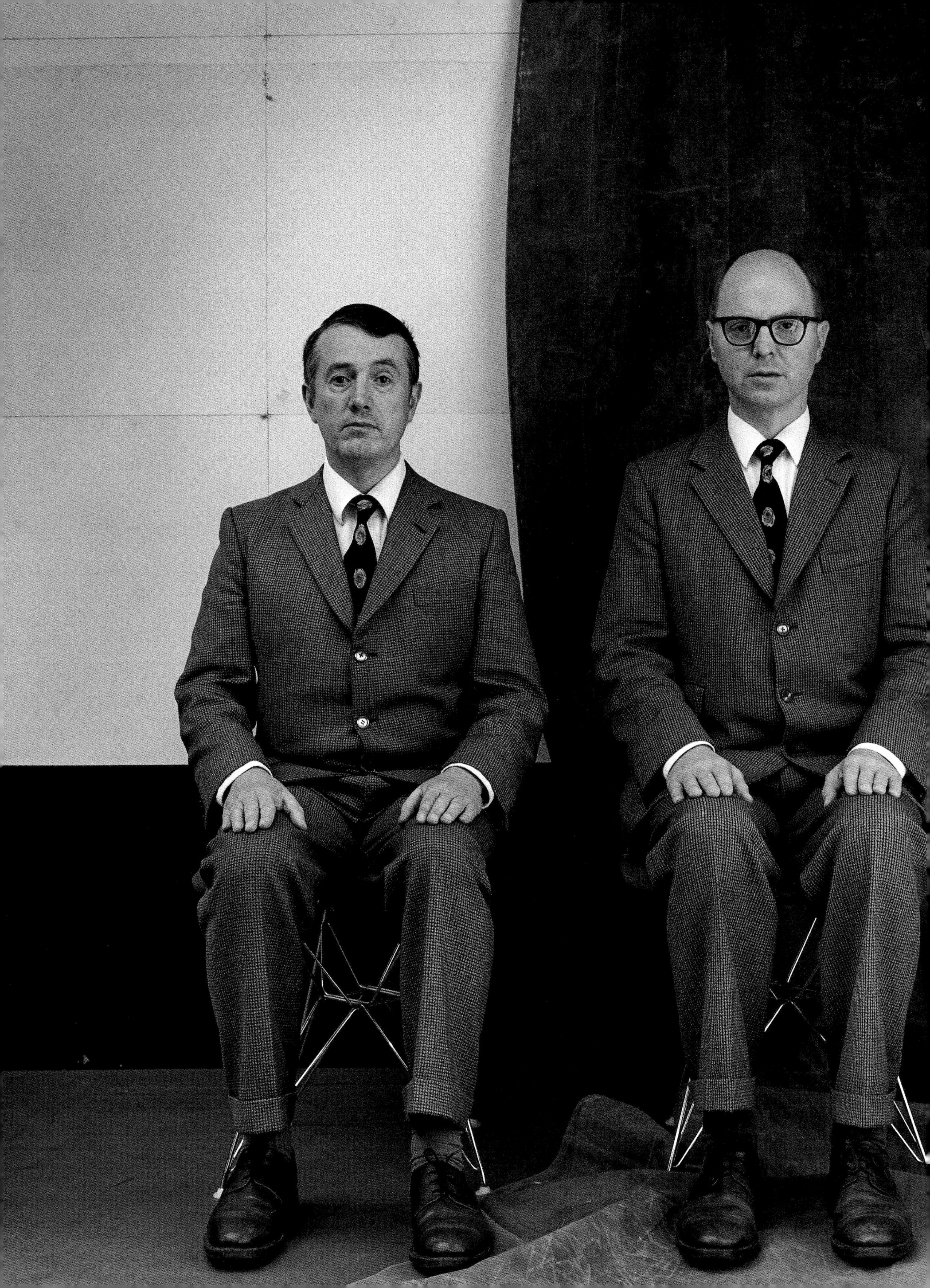

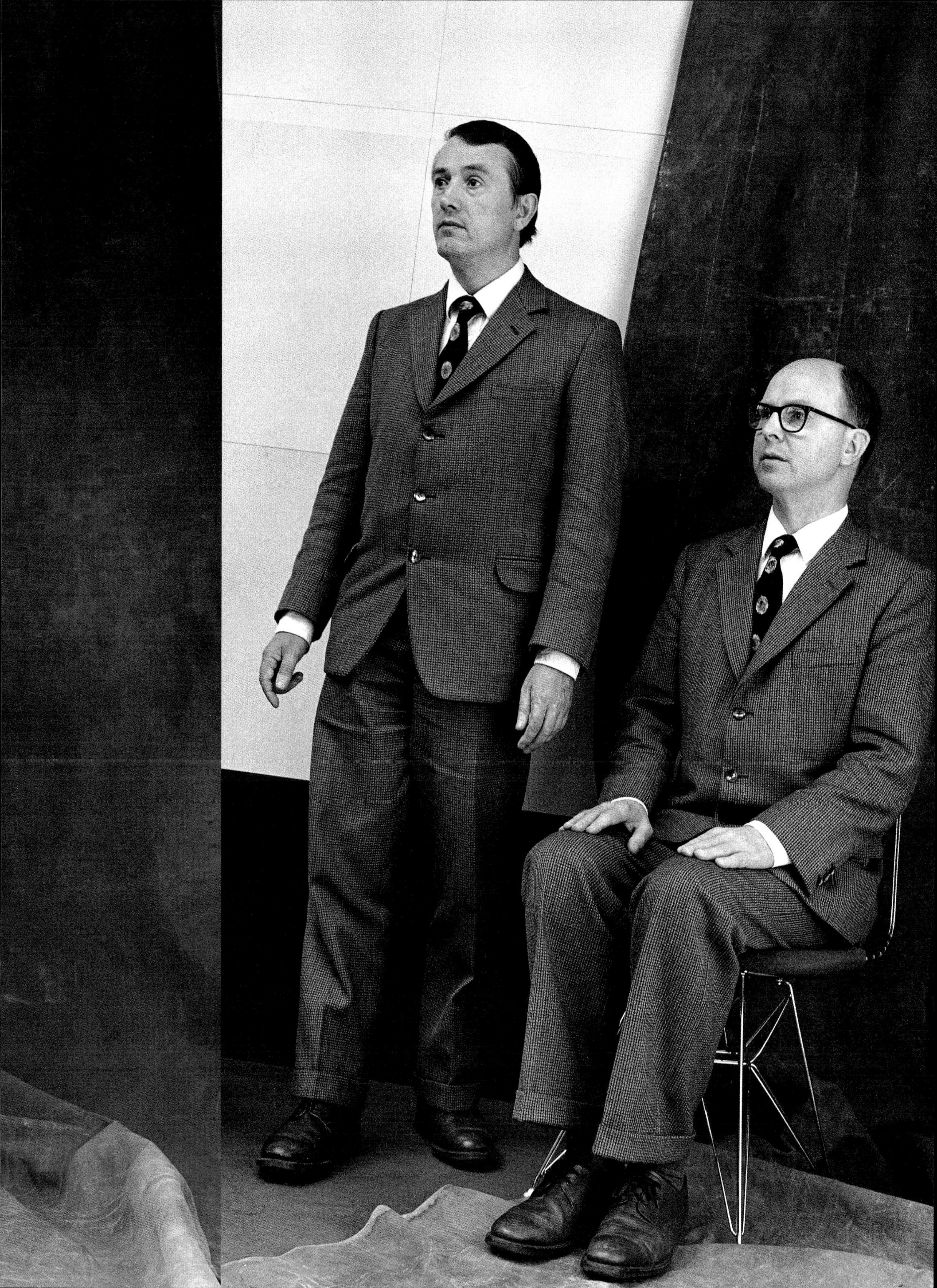

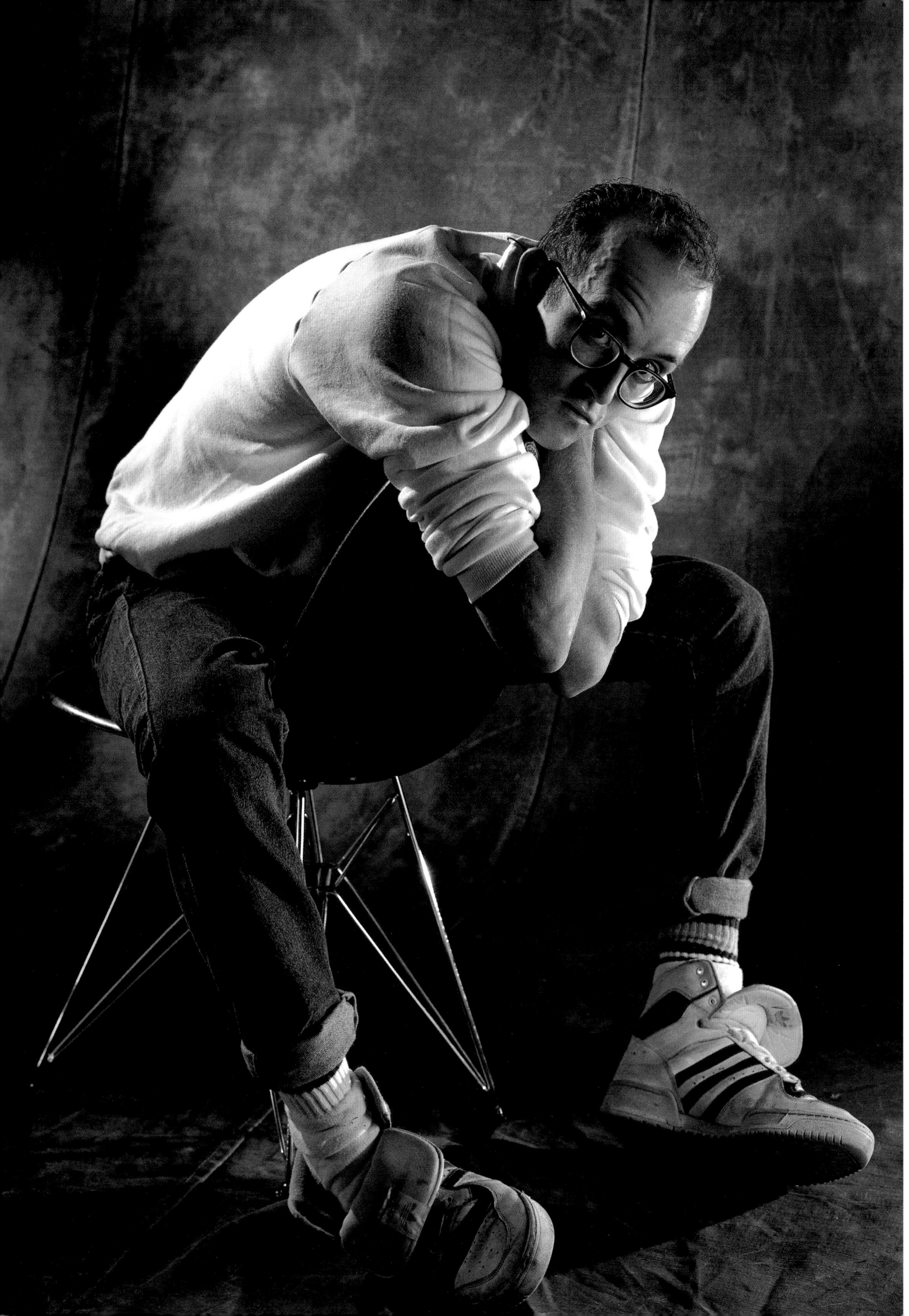

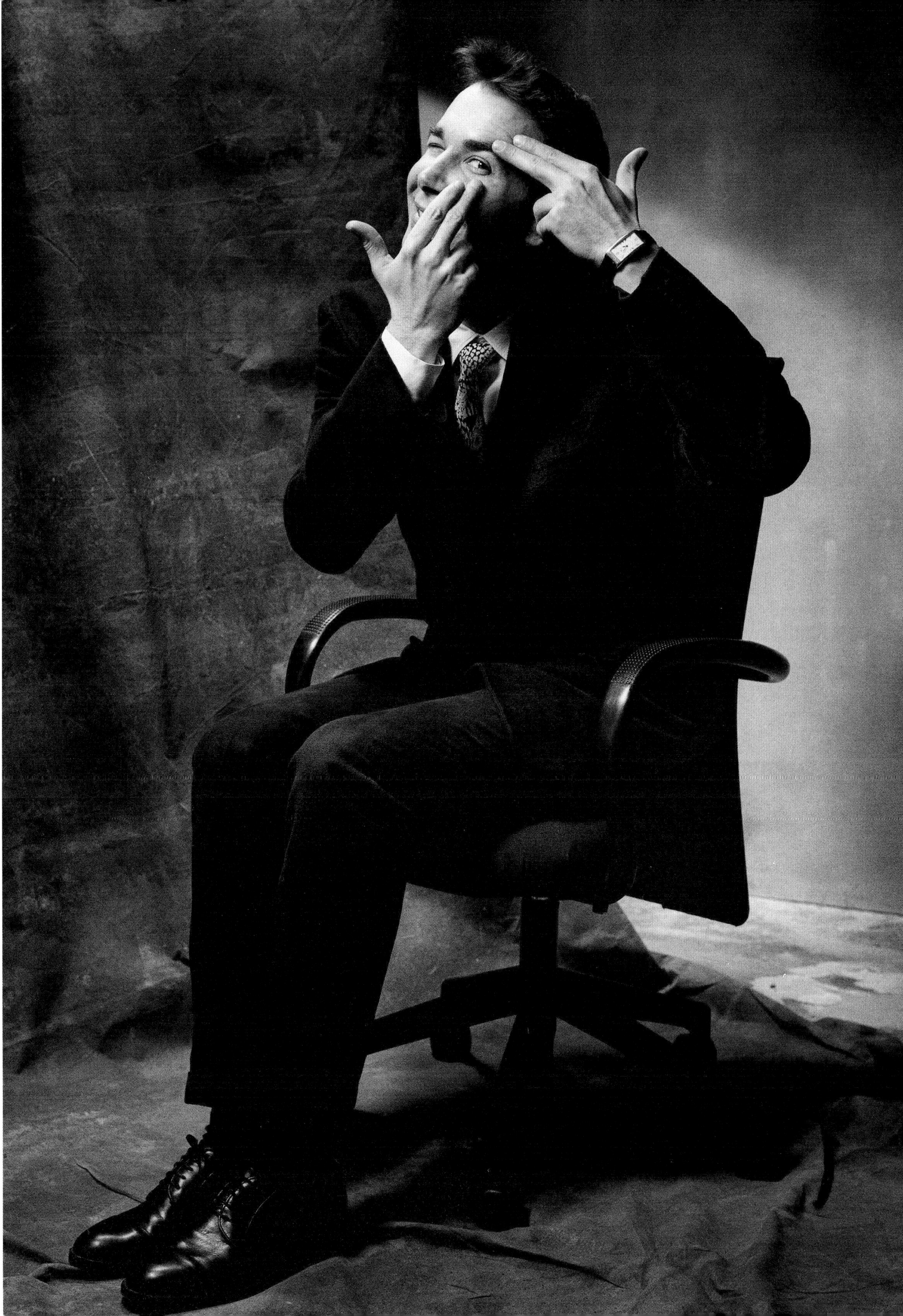

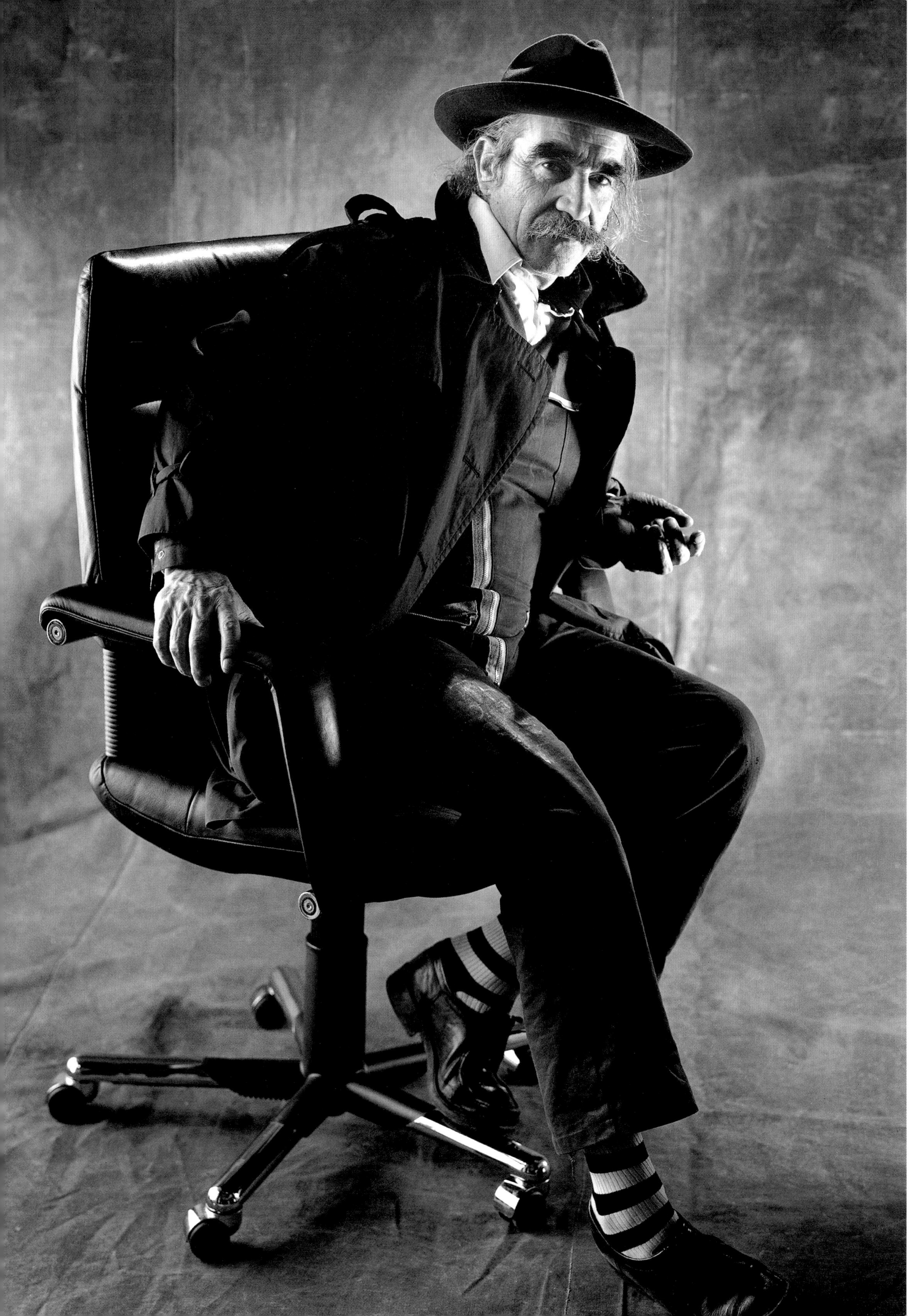

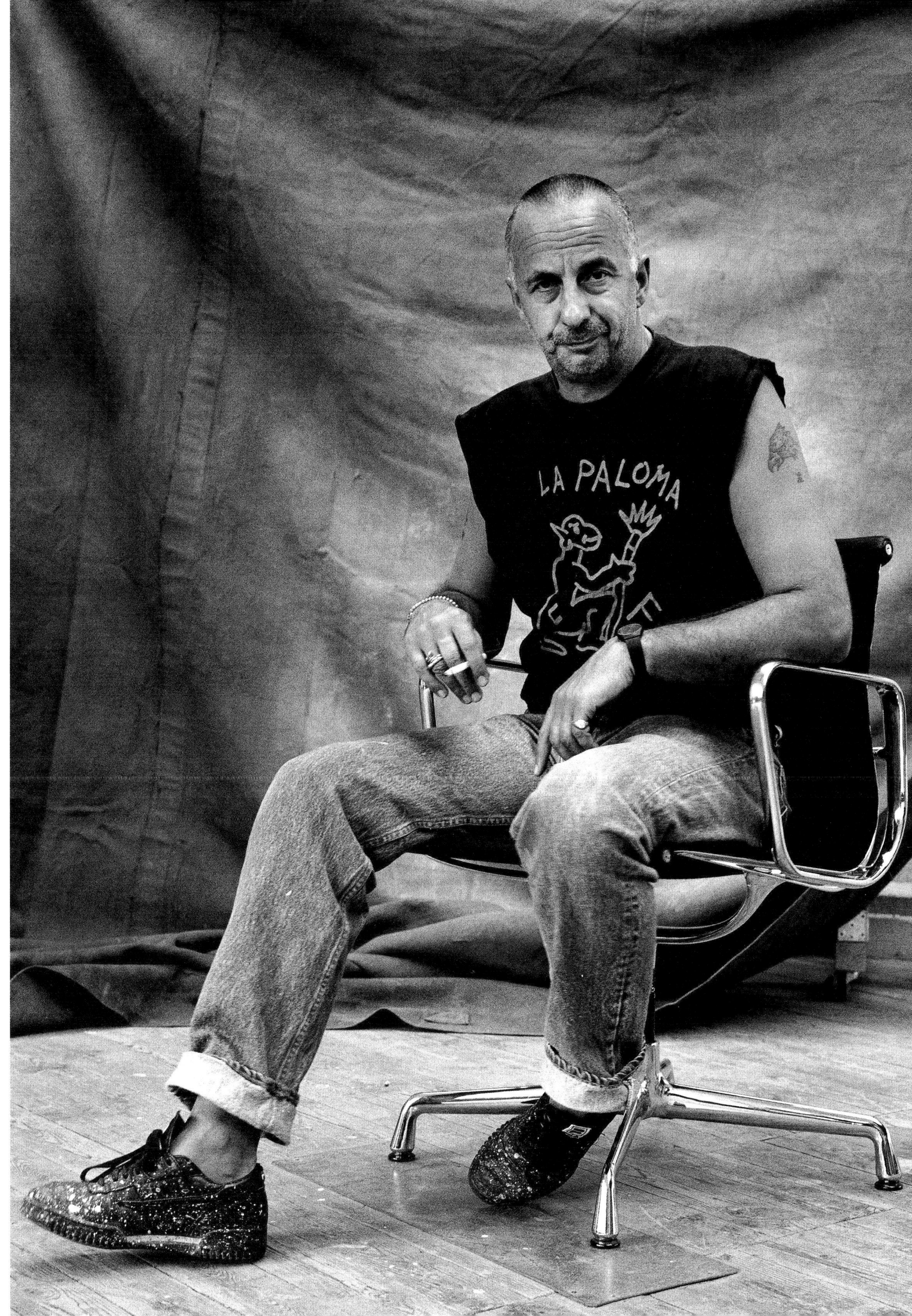
LA PALOMA

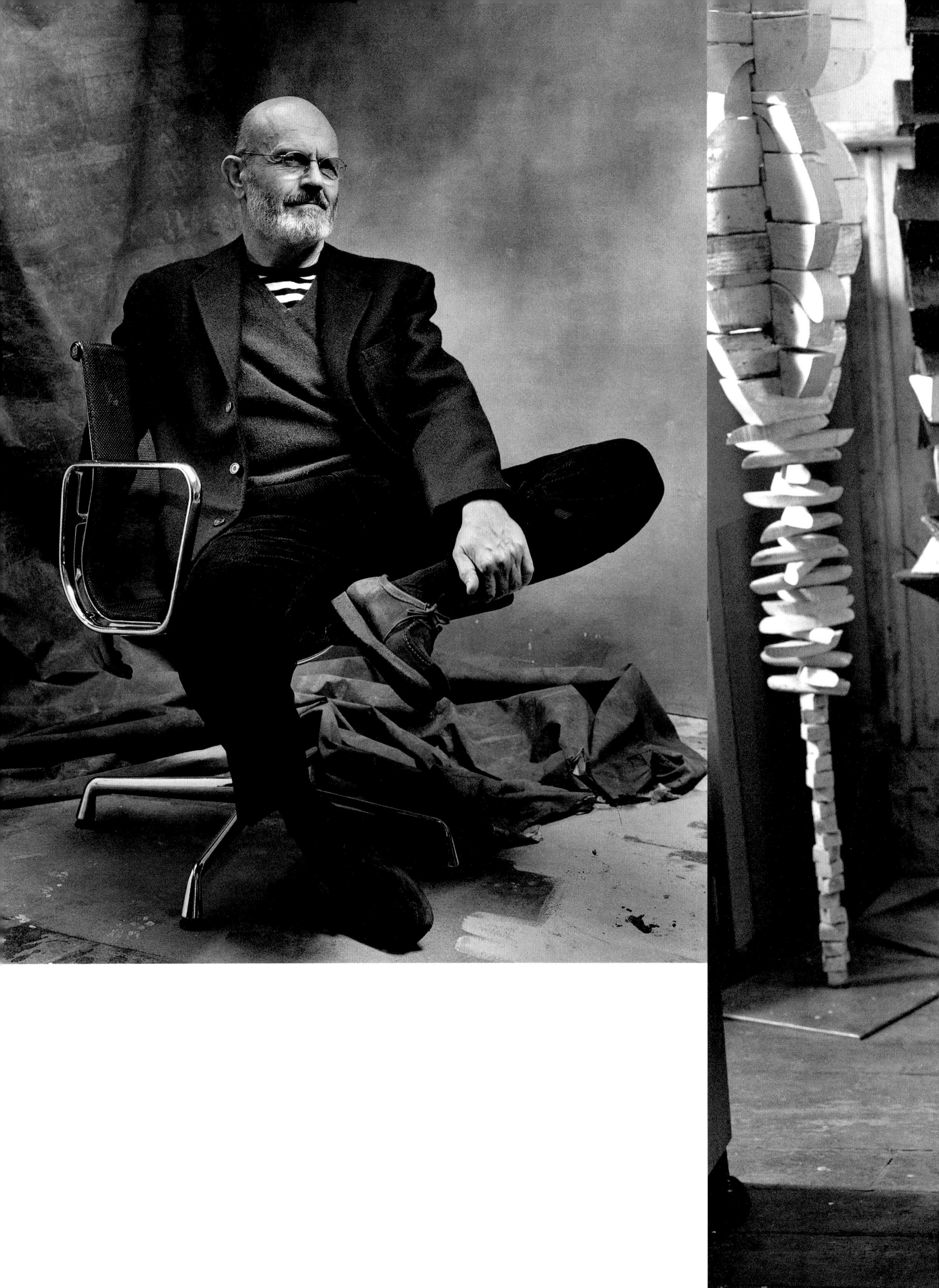

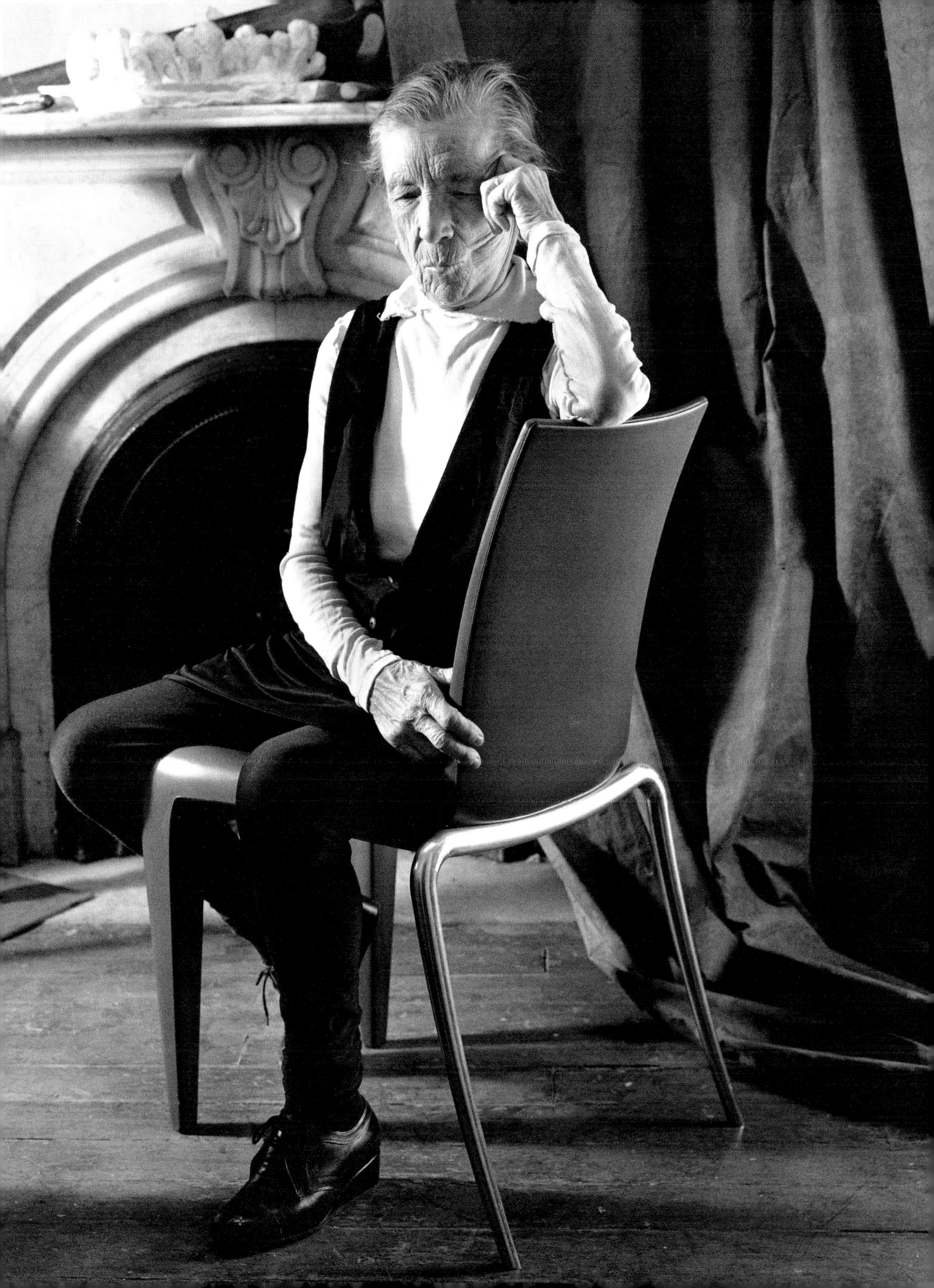

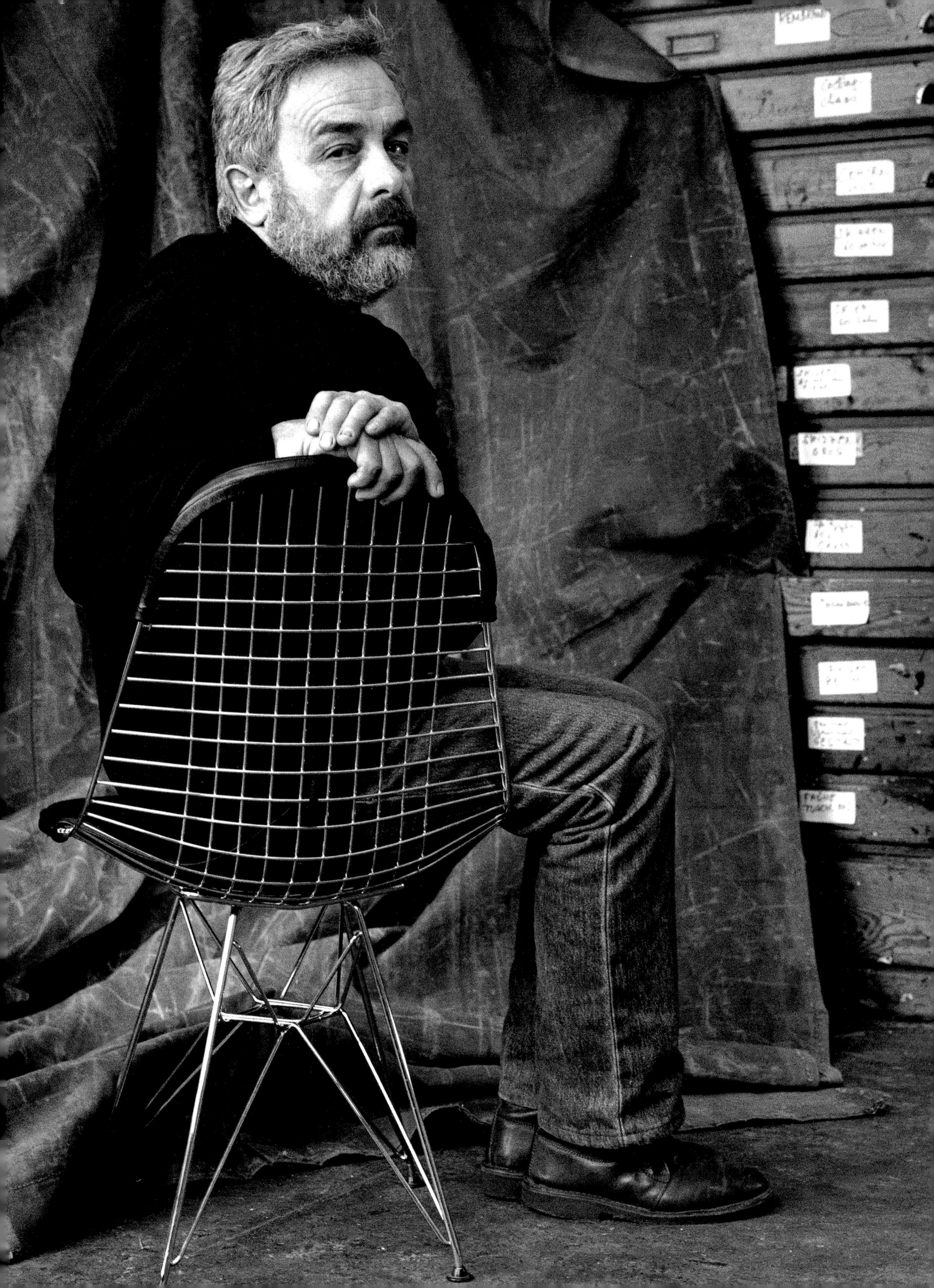

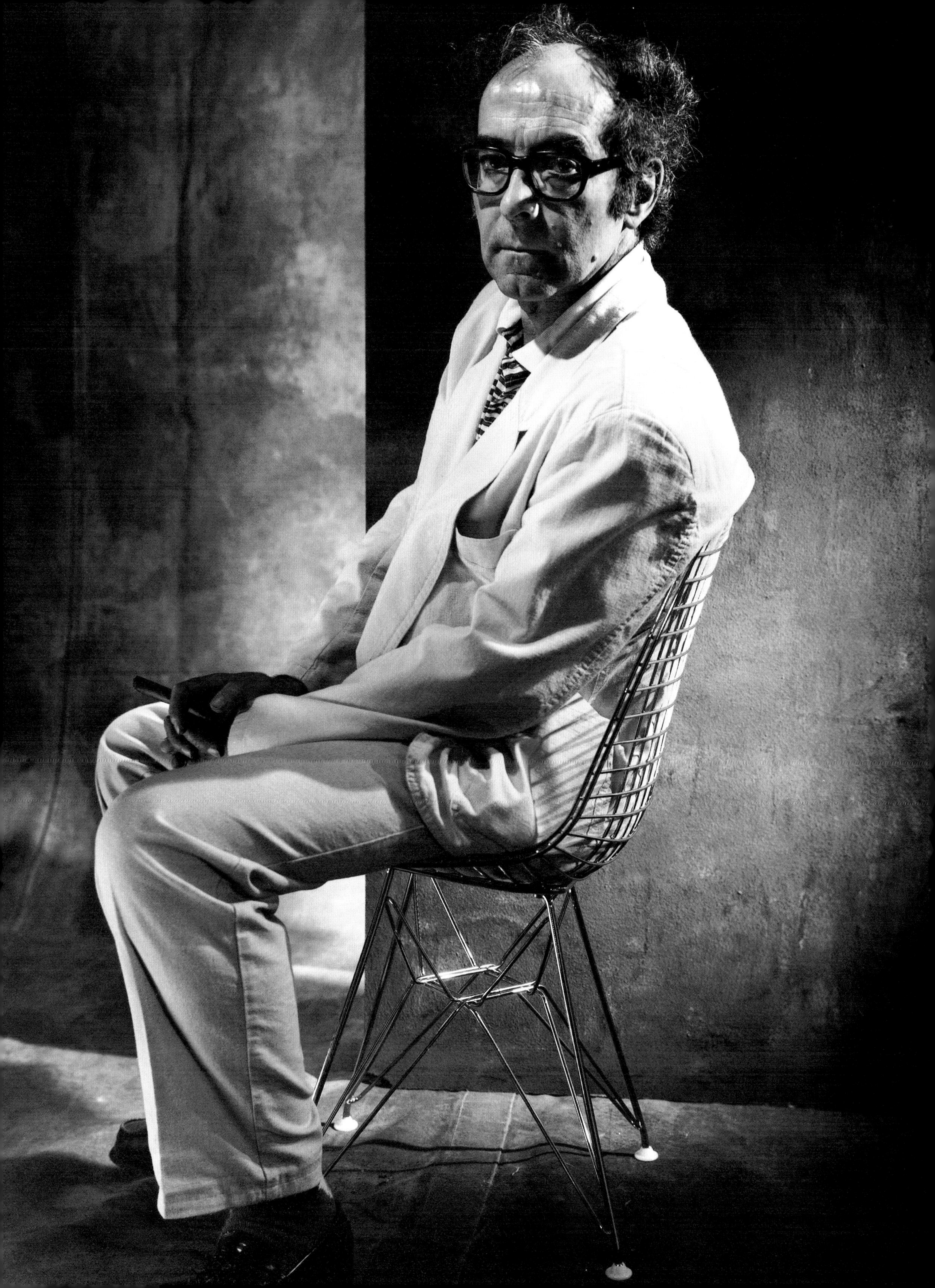

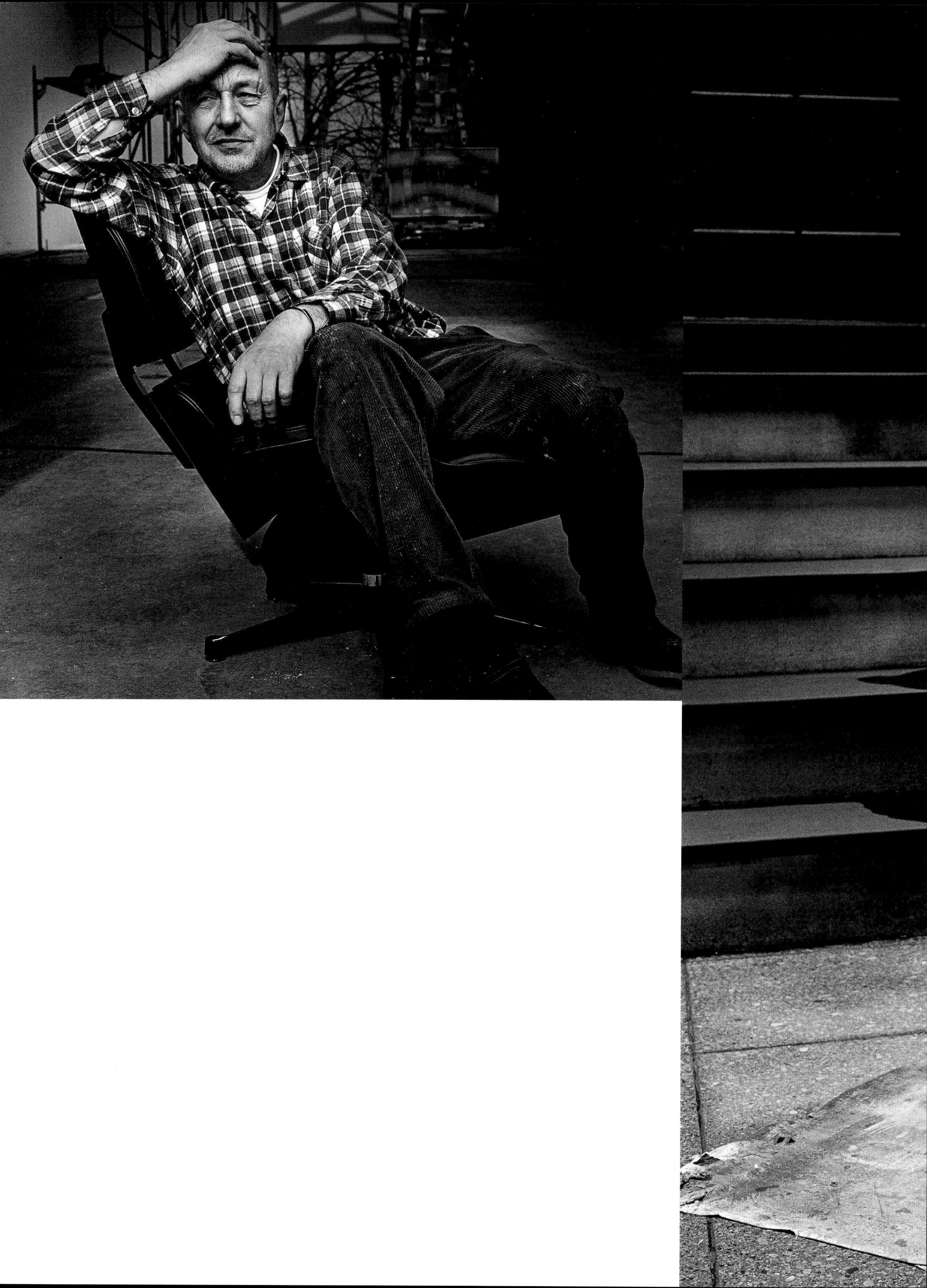

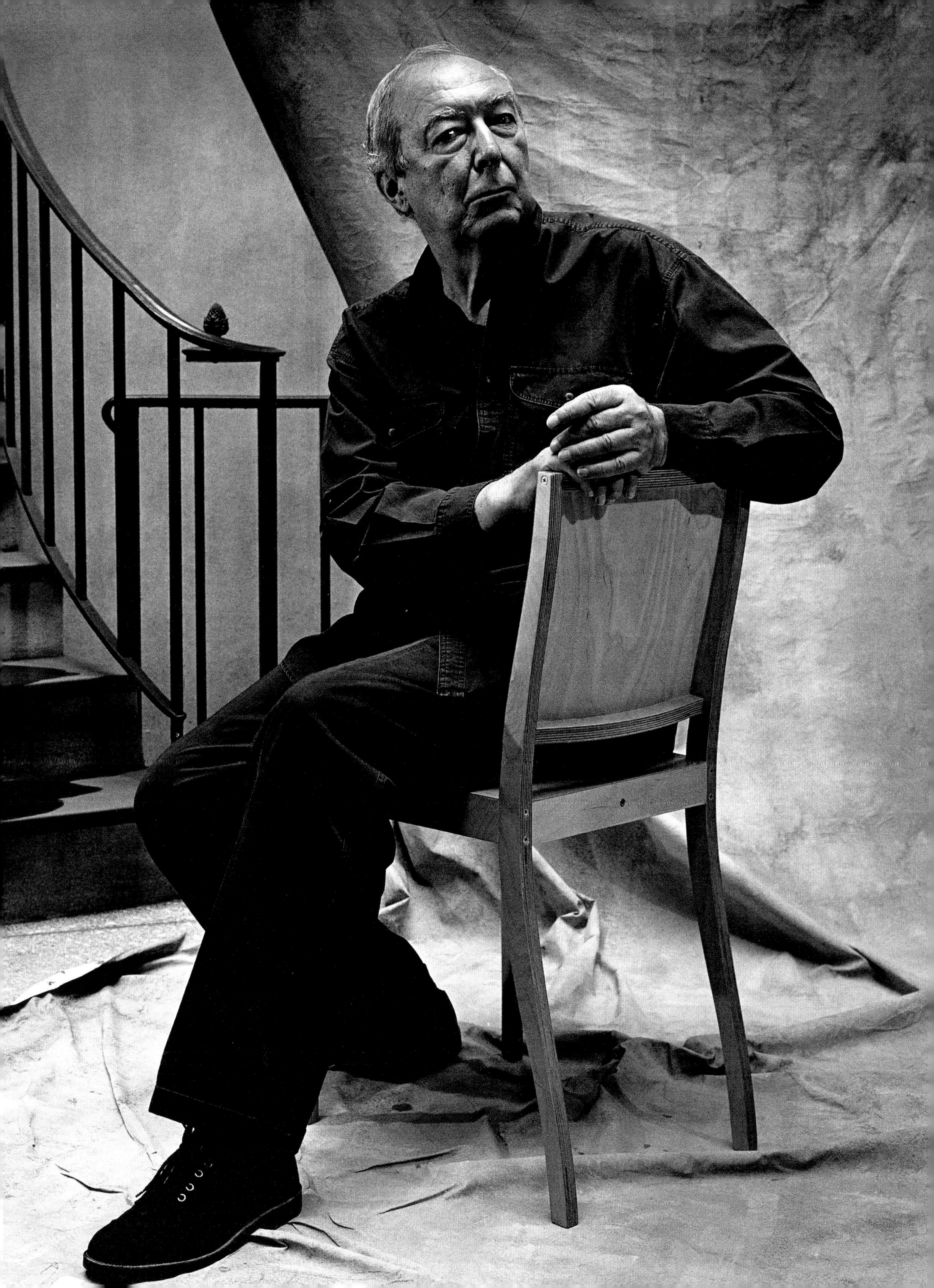

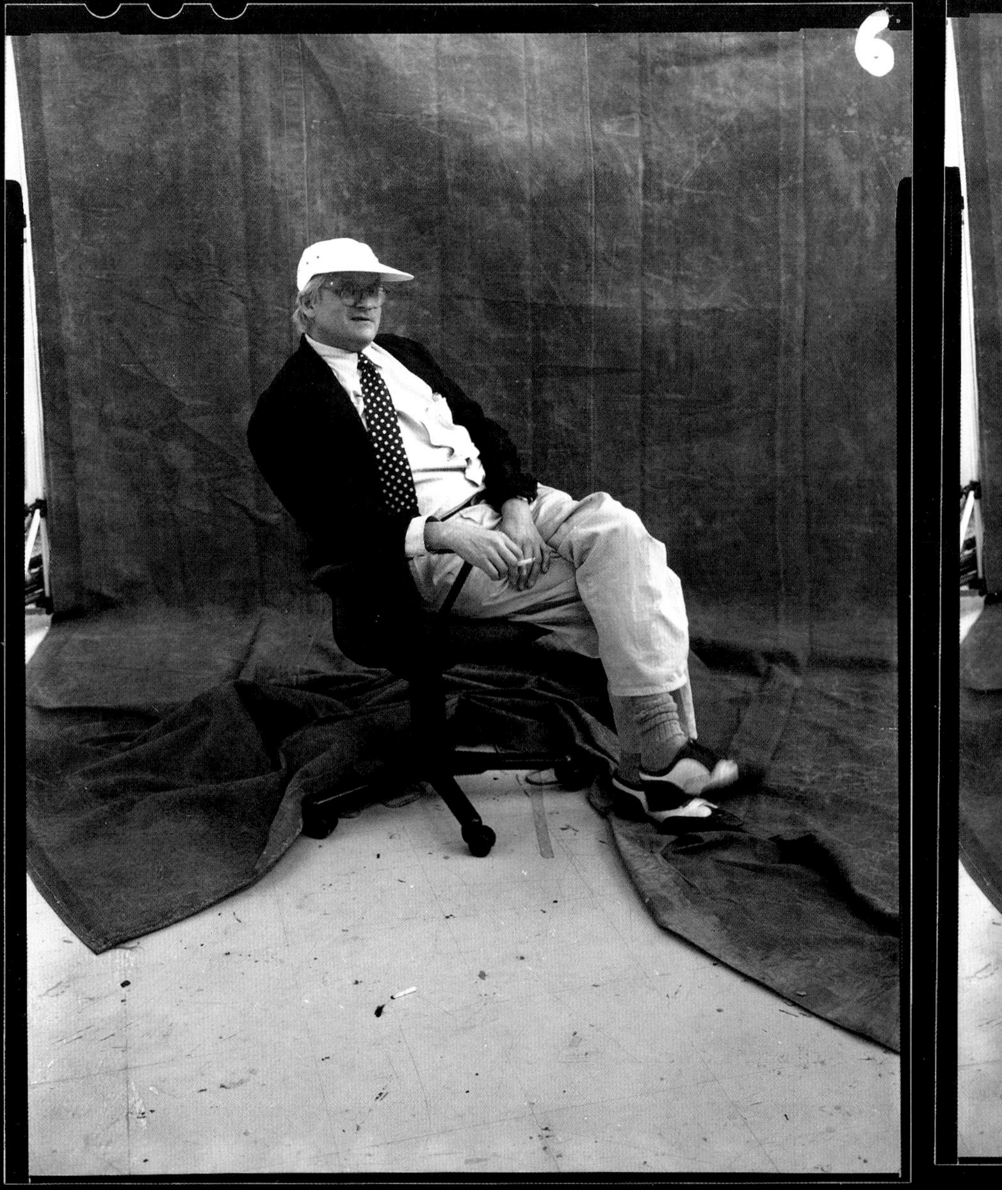

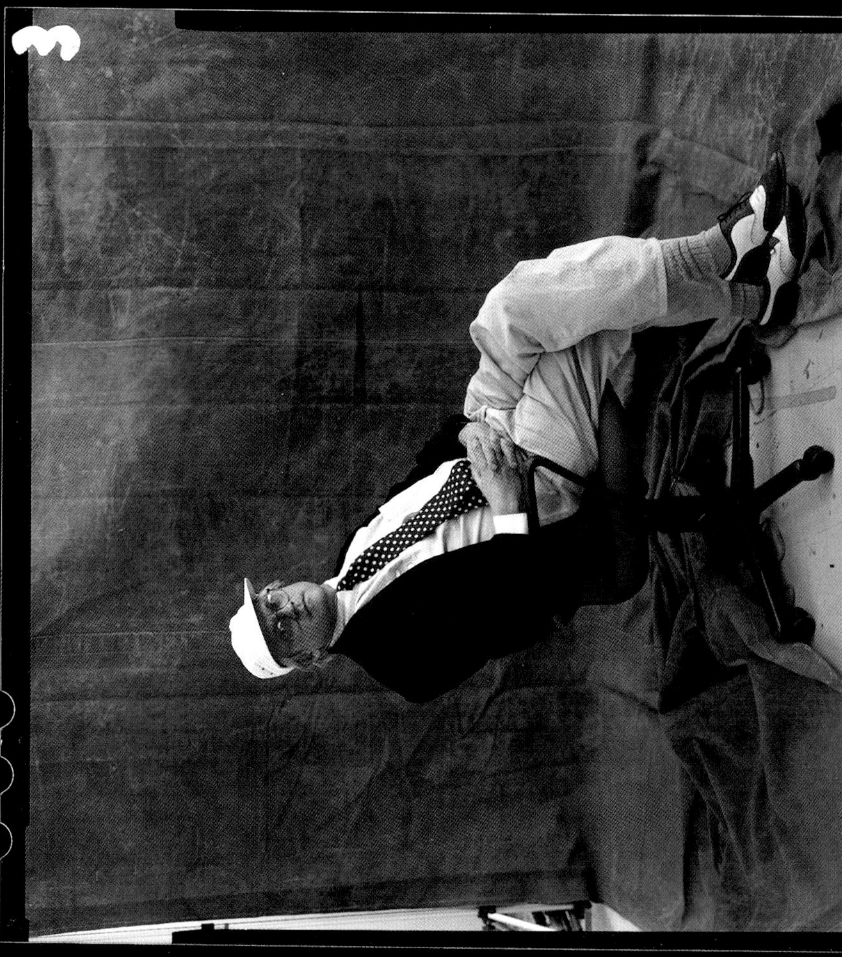

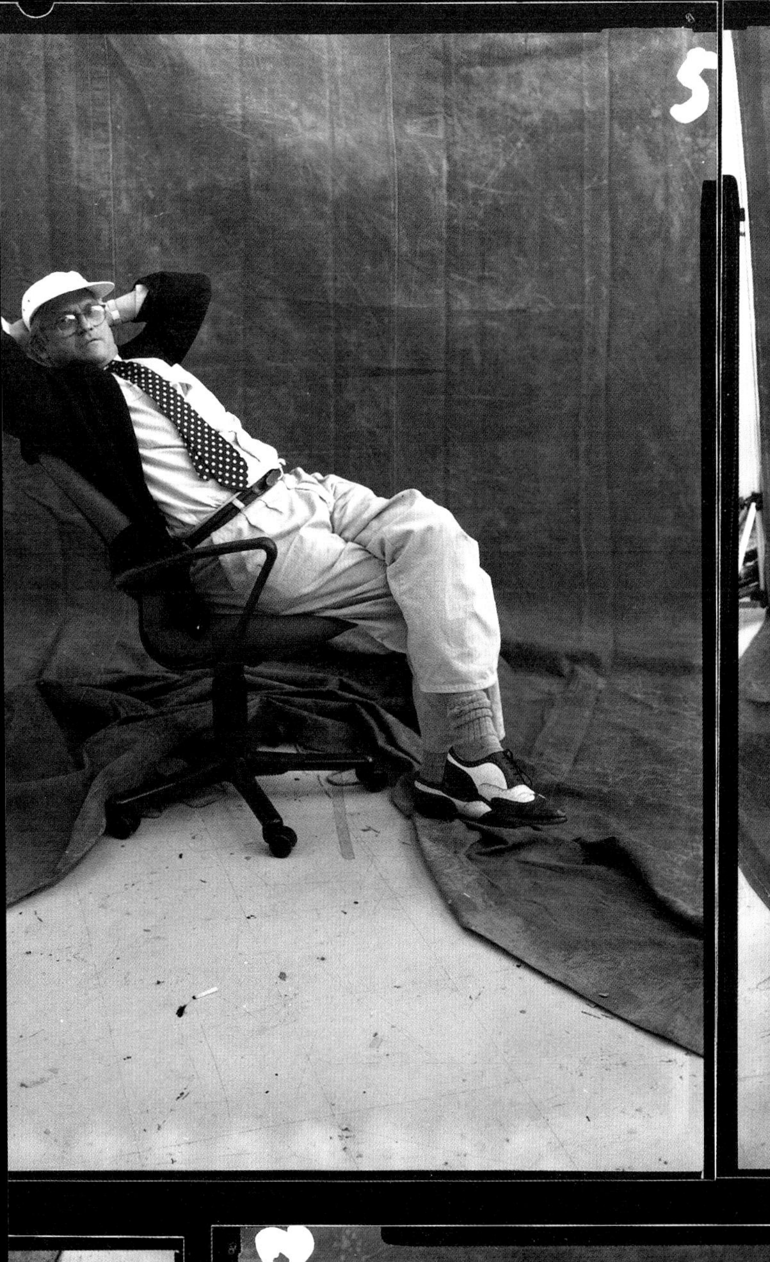
5

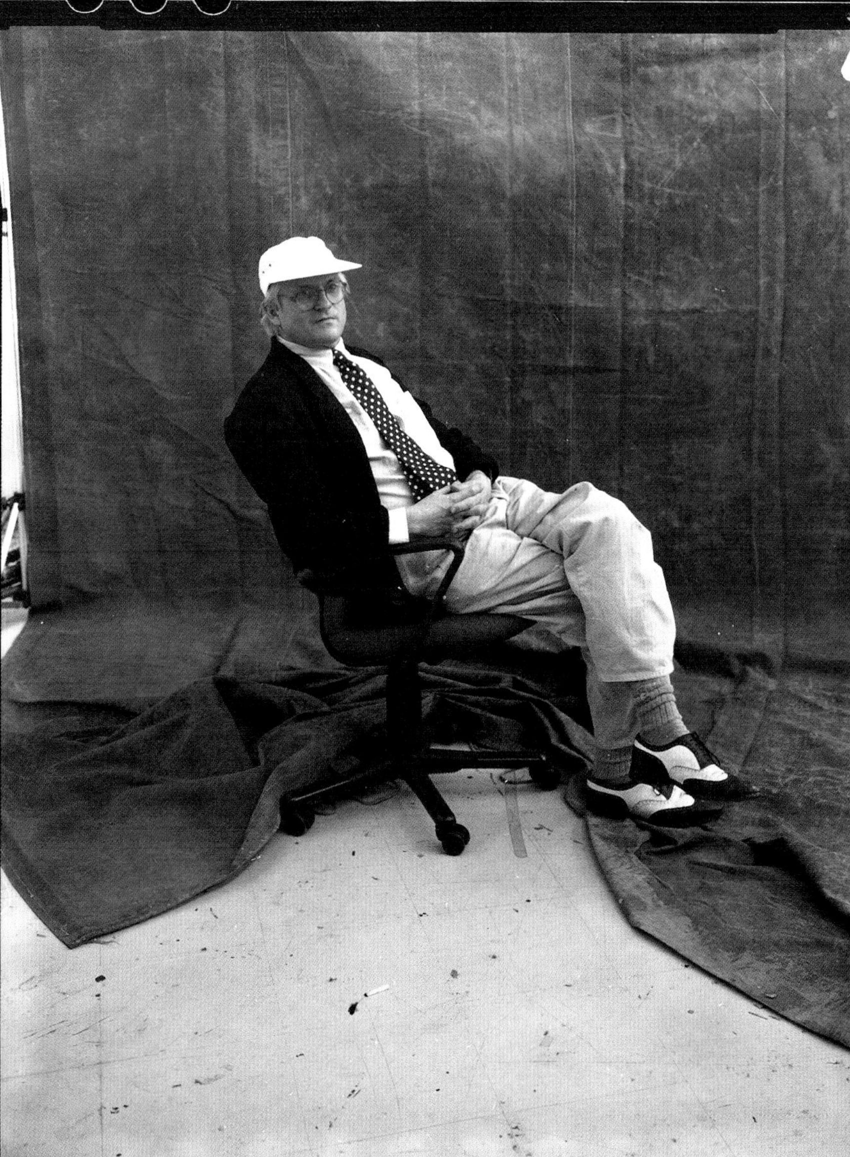

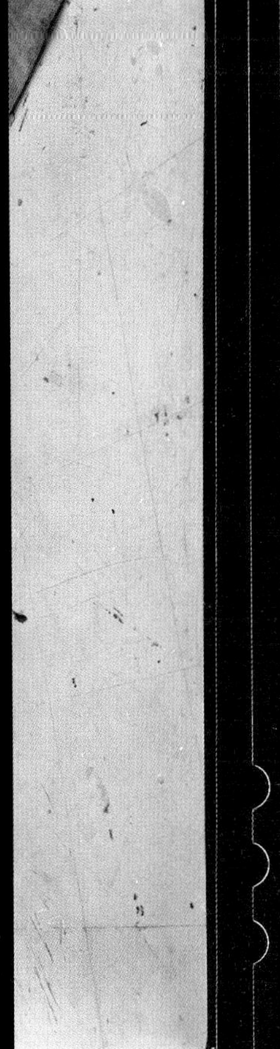

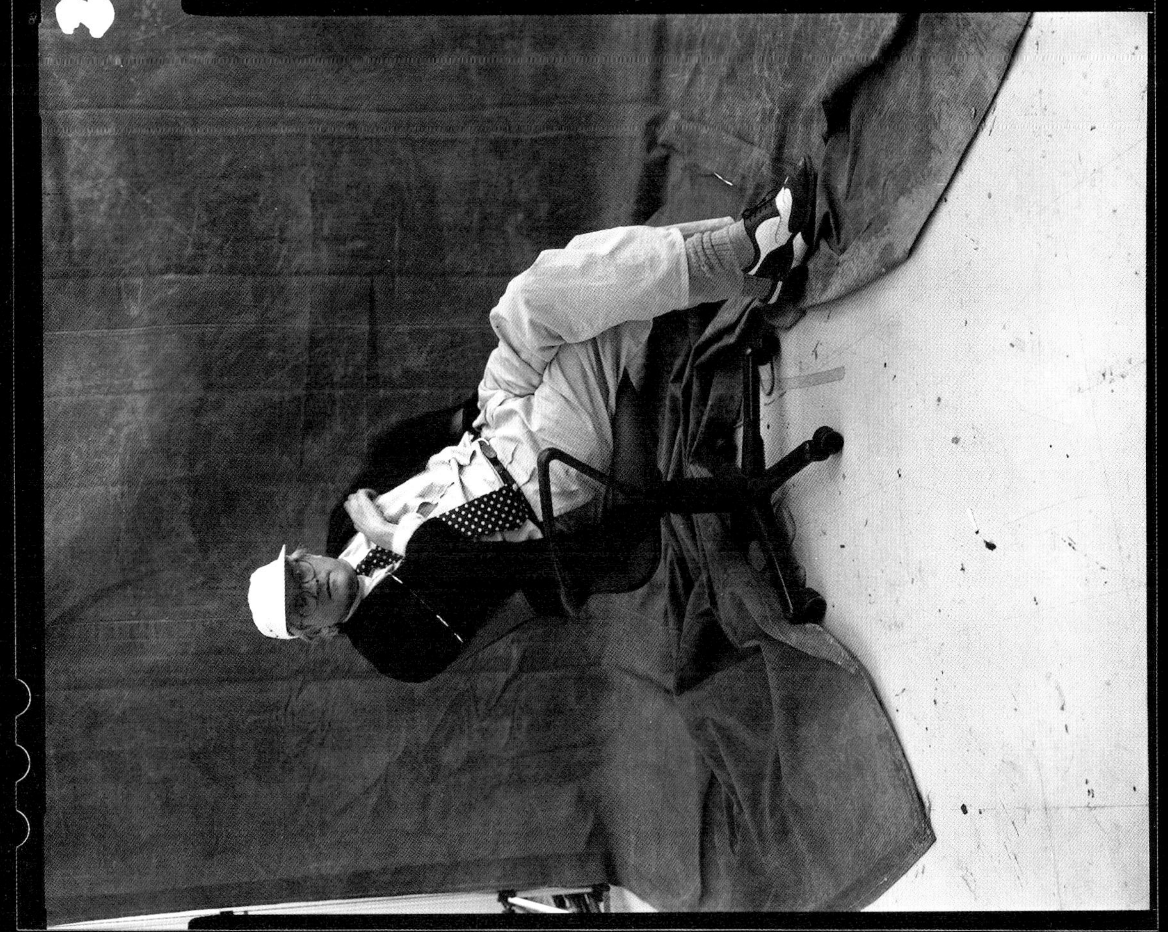

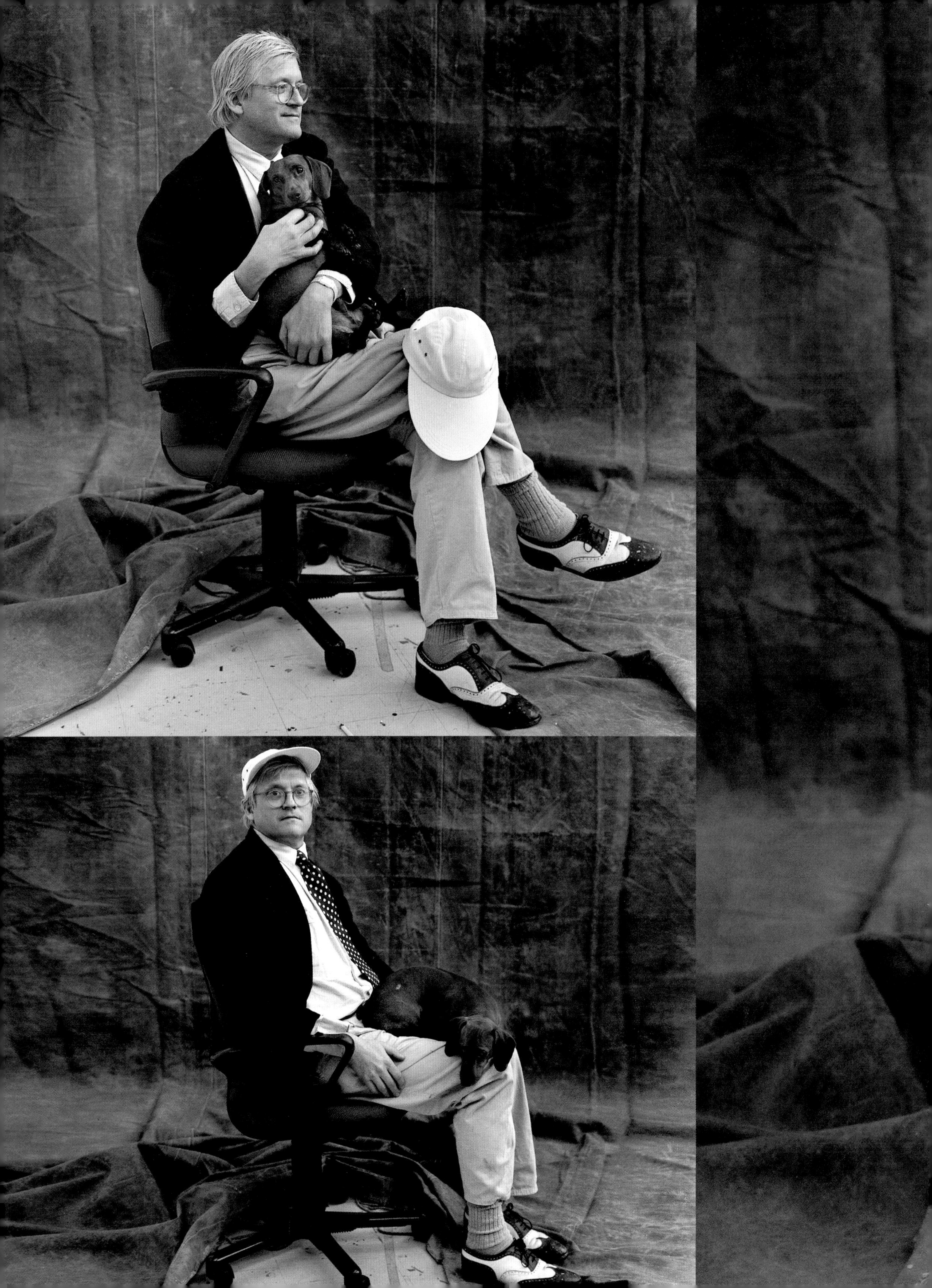

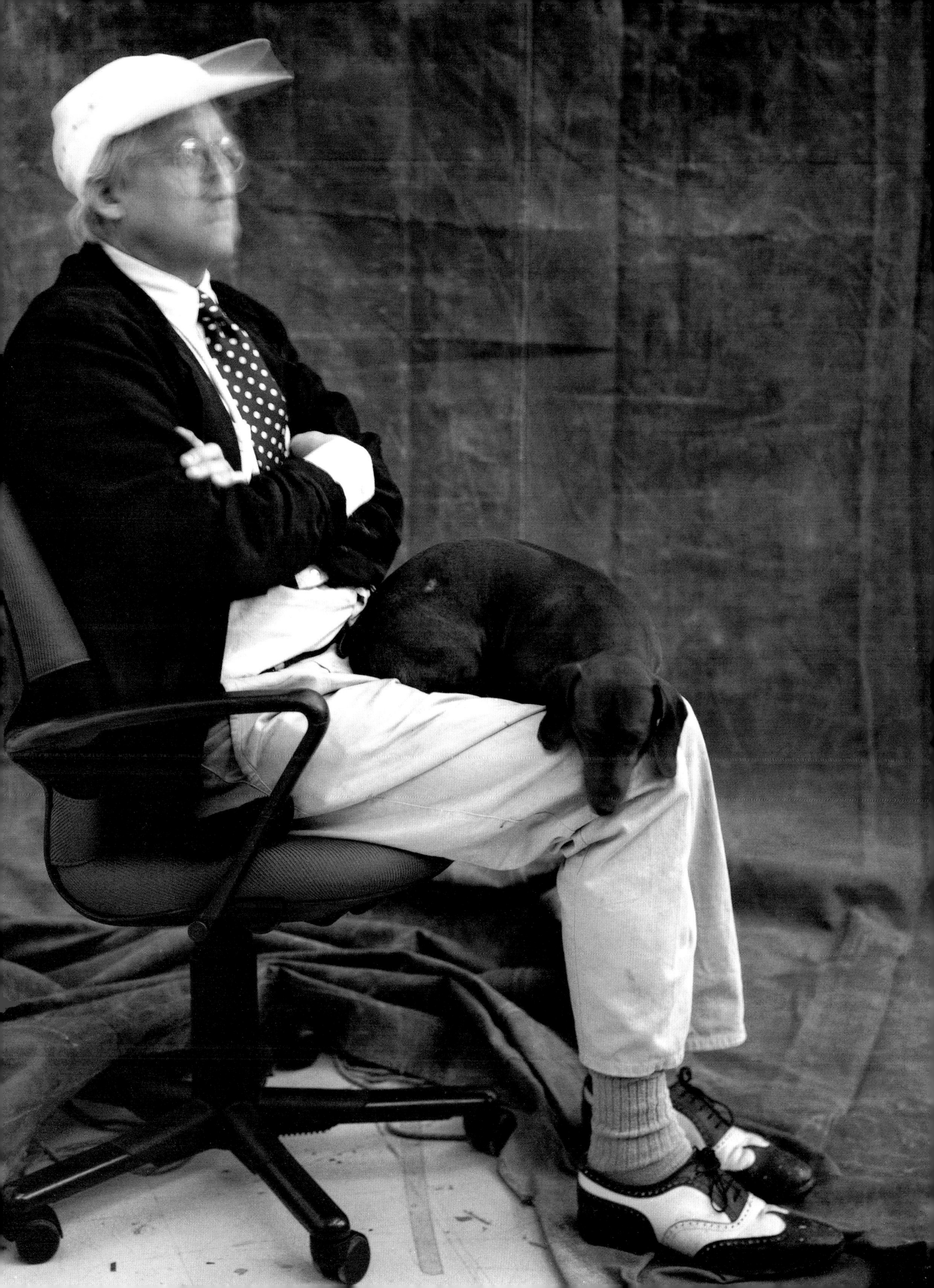

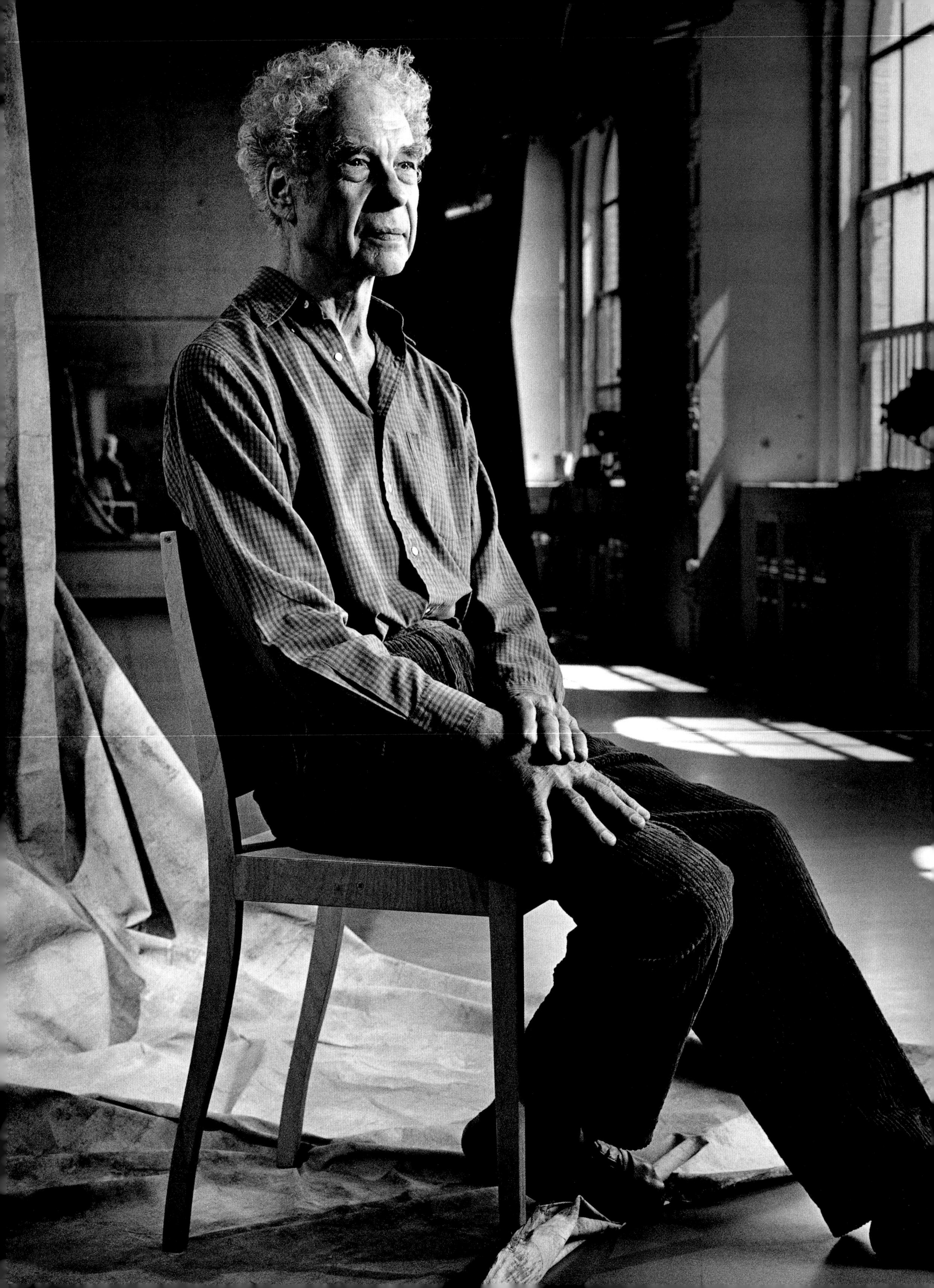

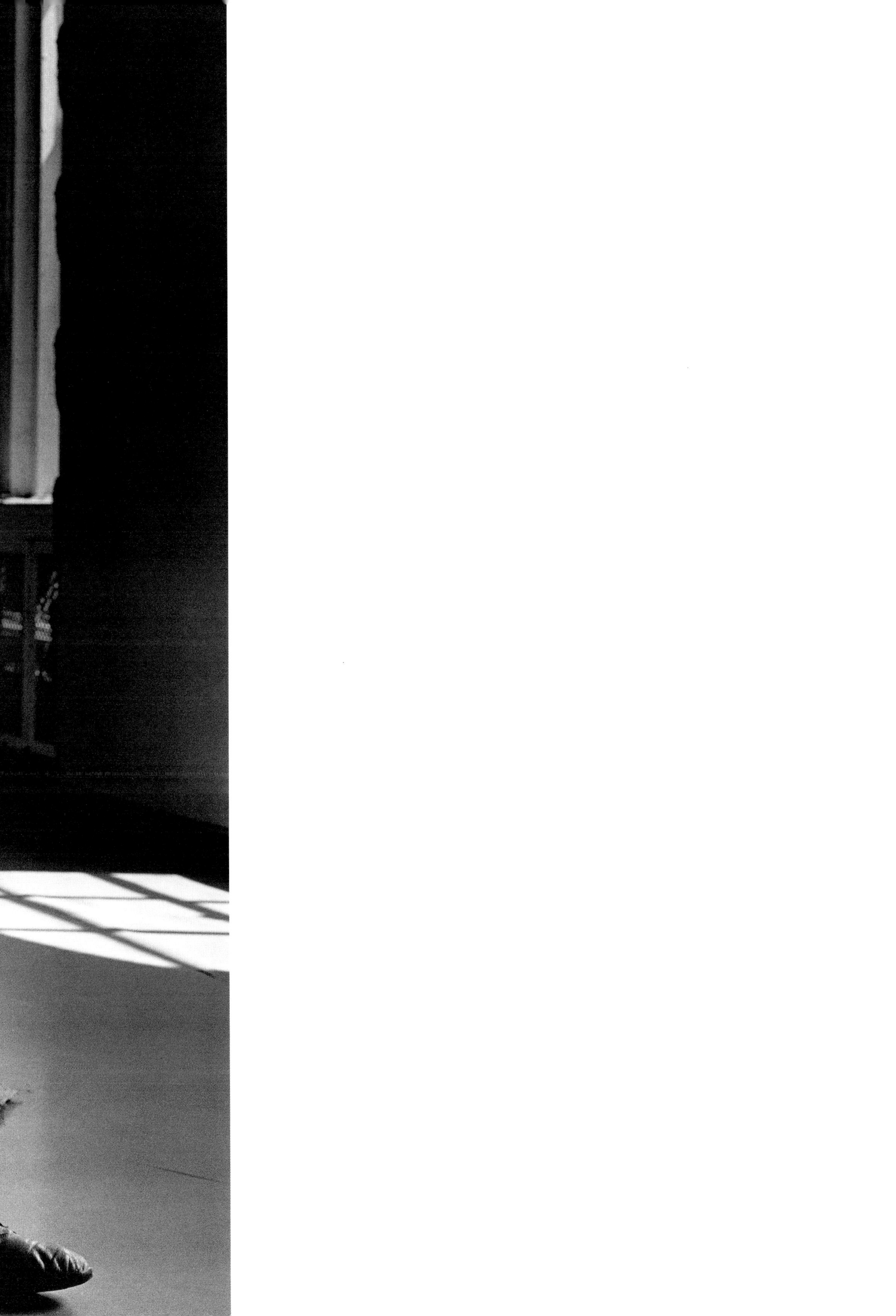

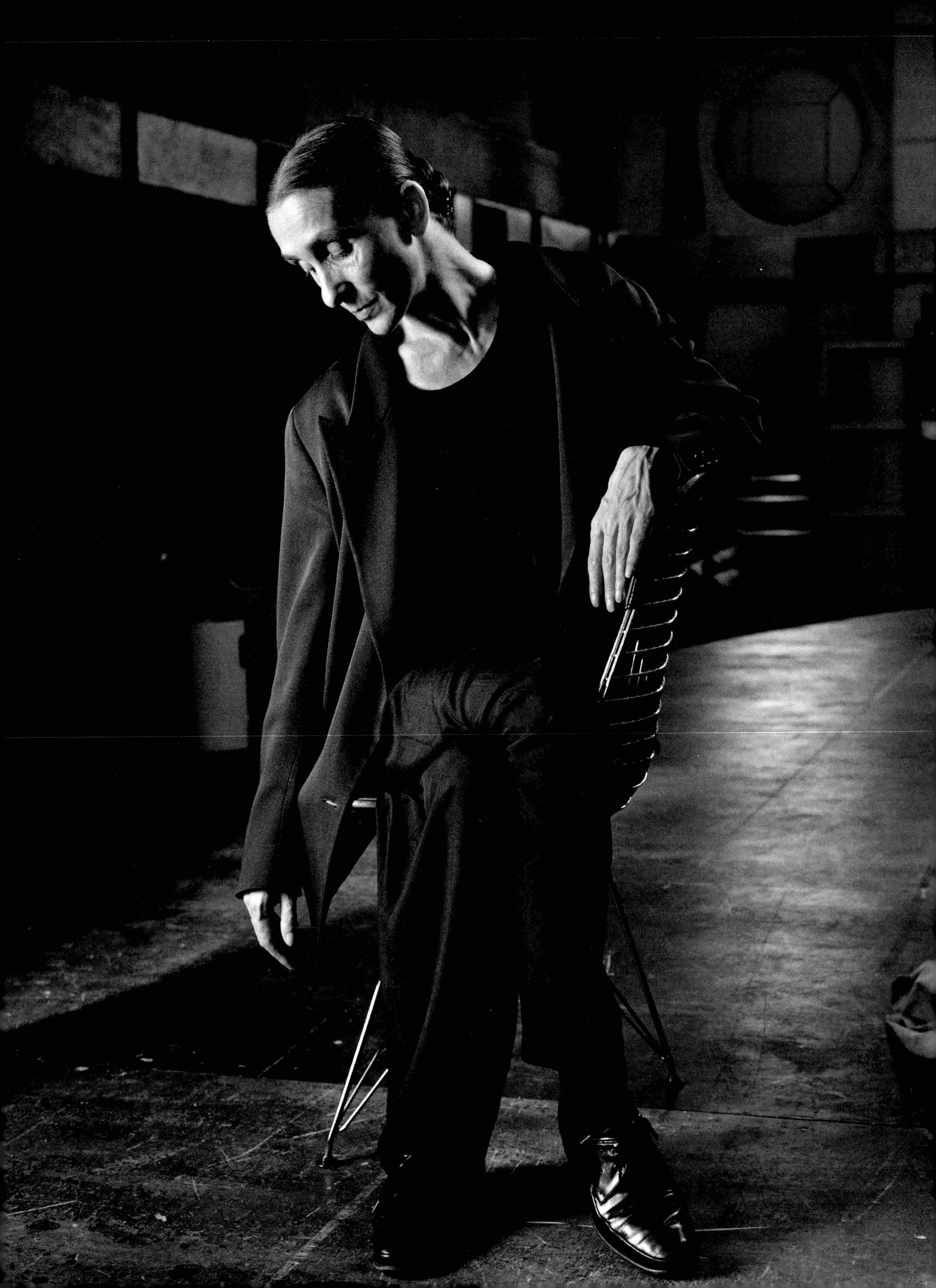

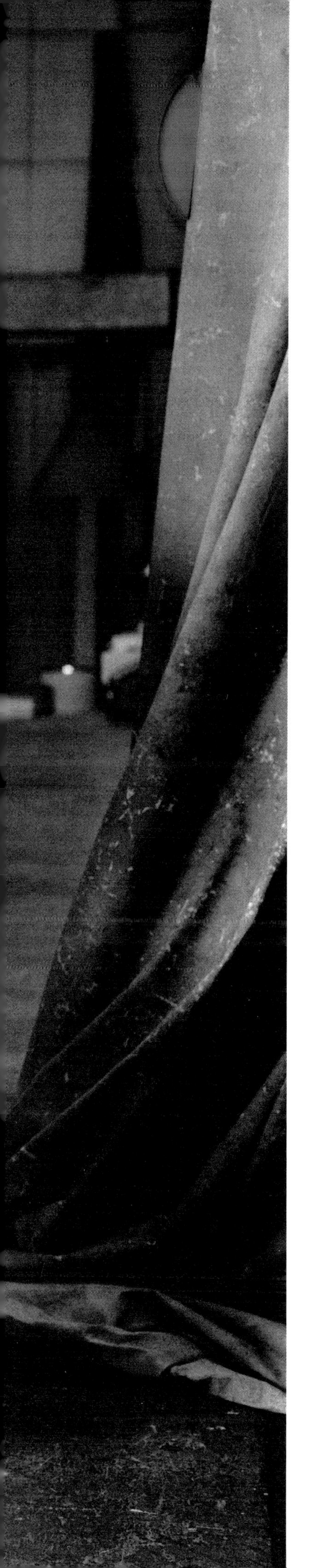

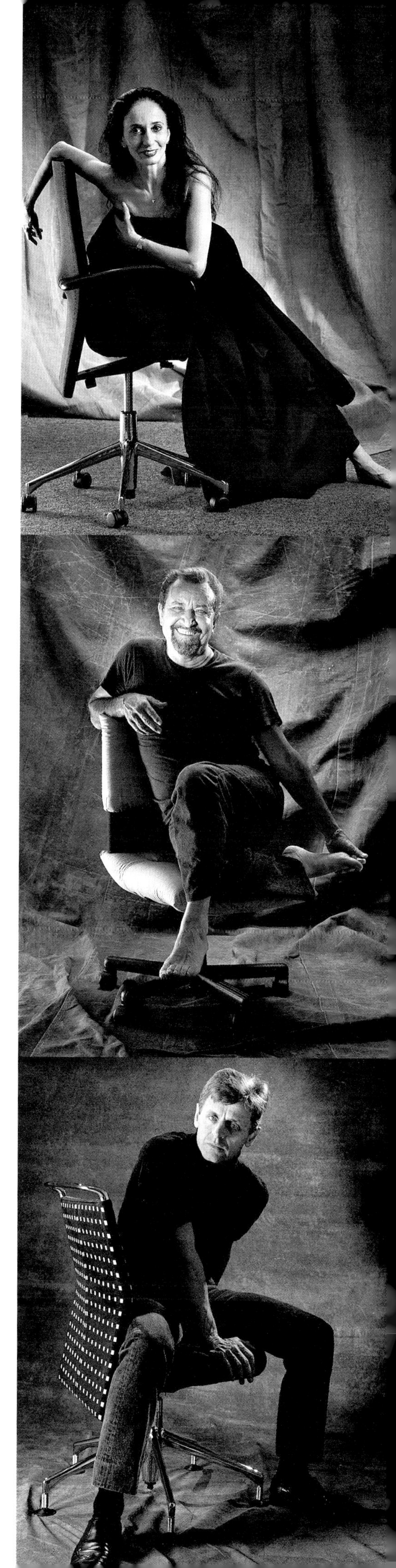

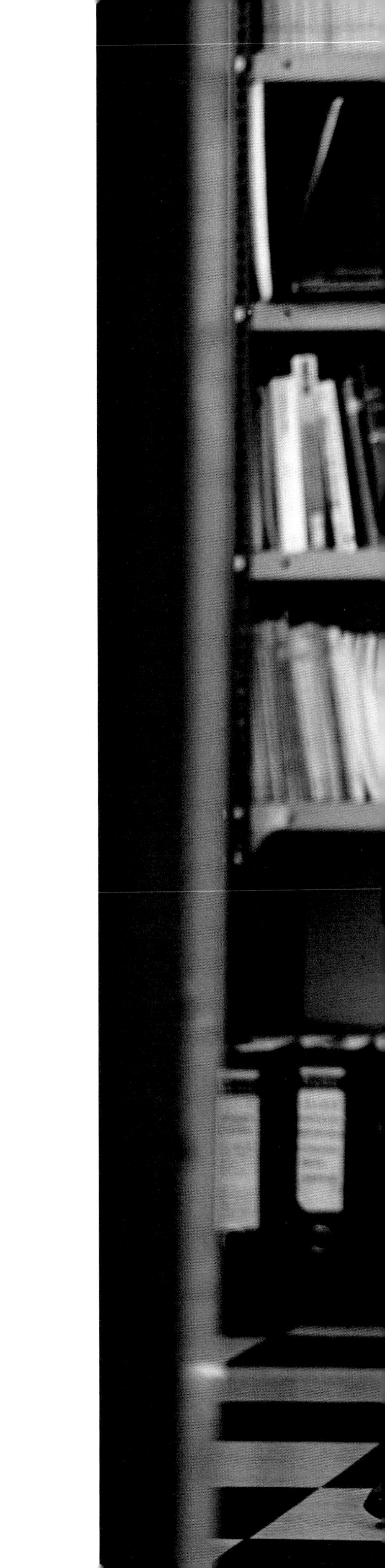

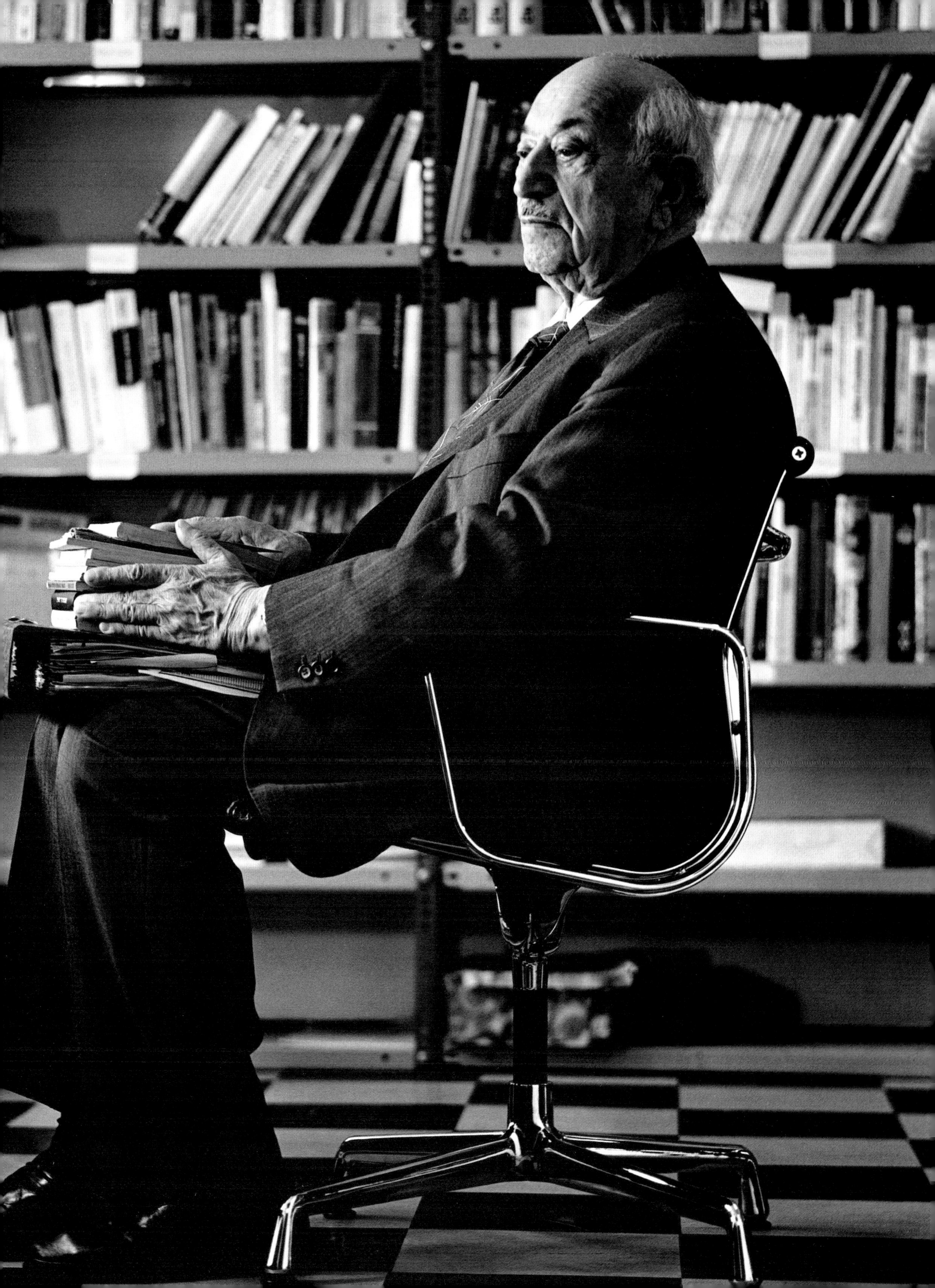

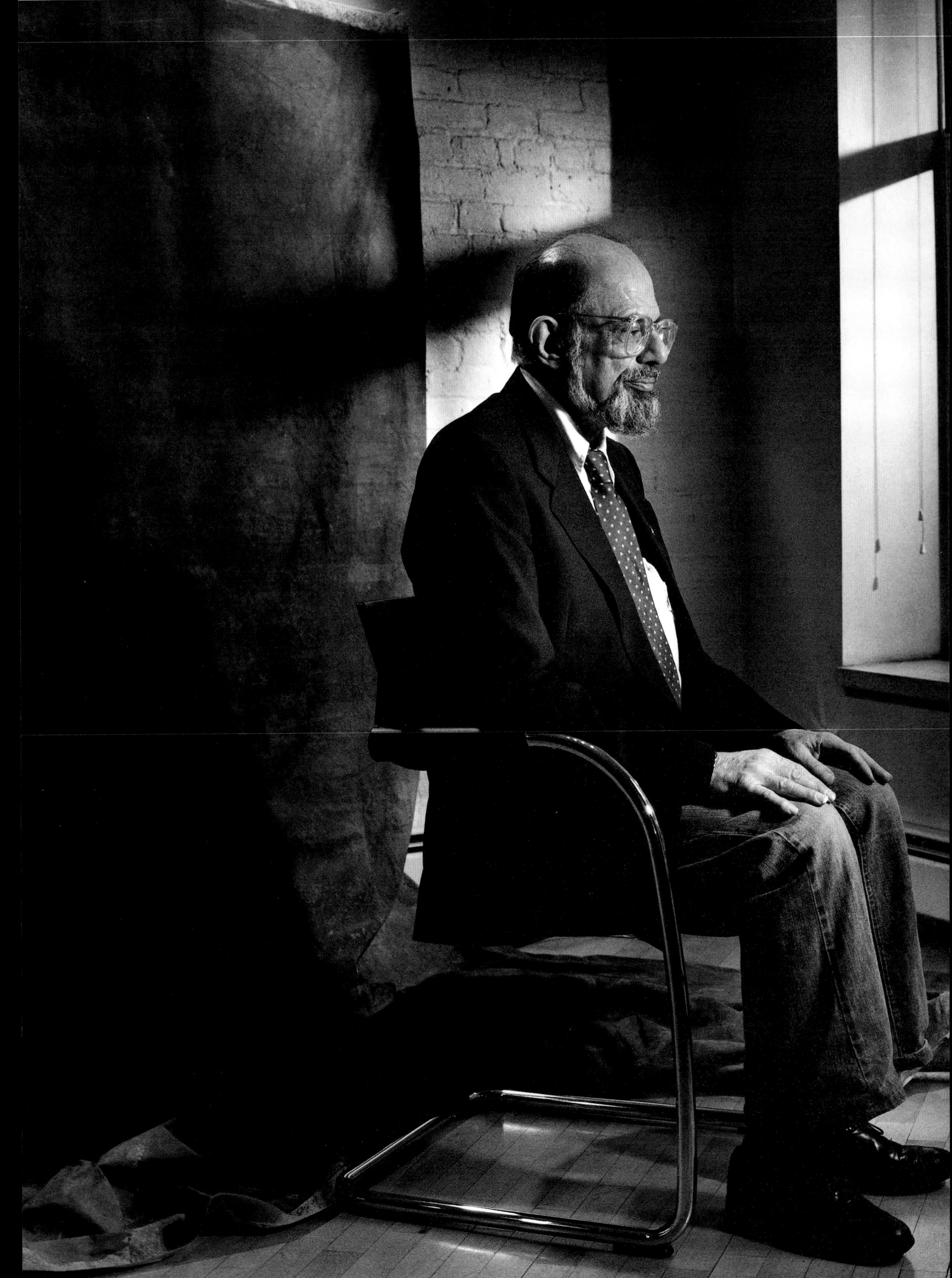

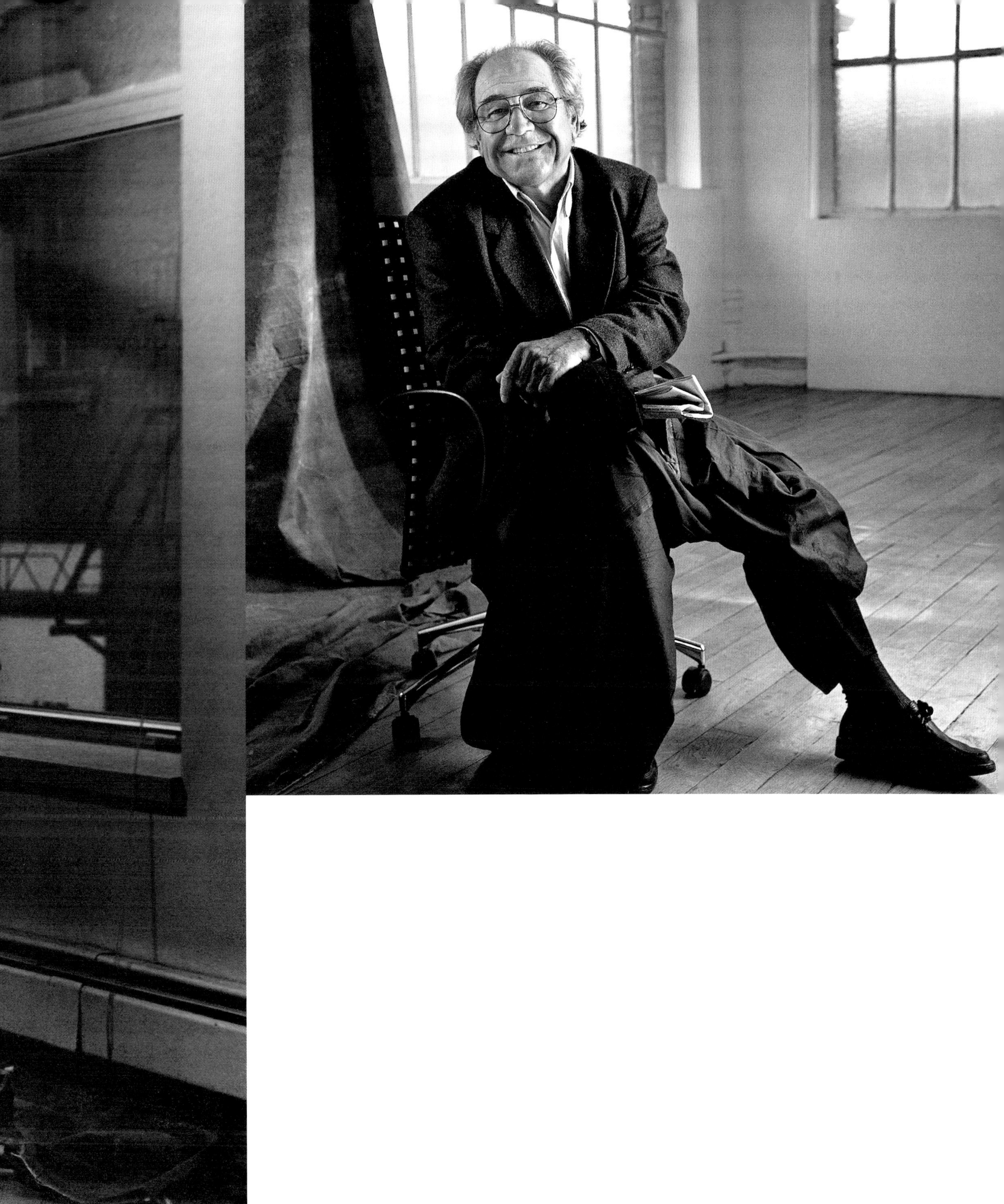

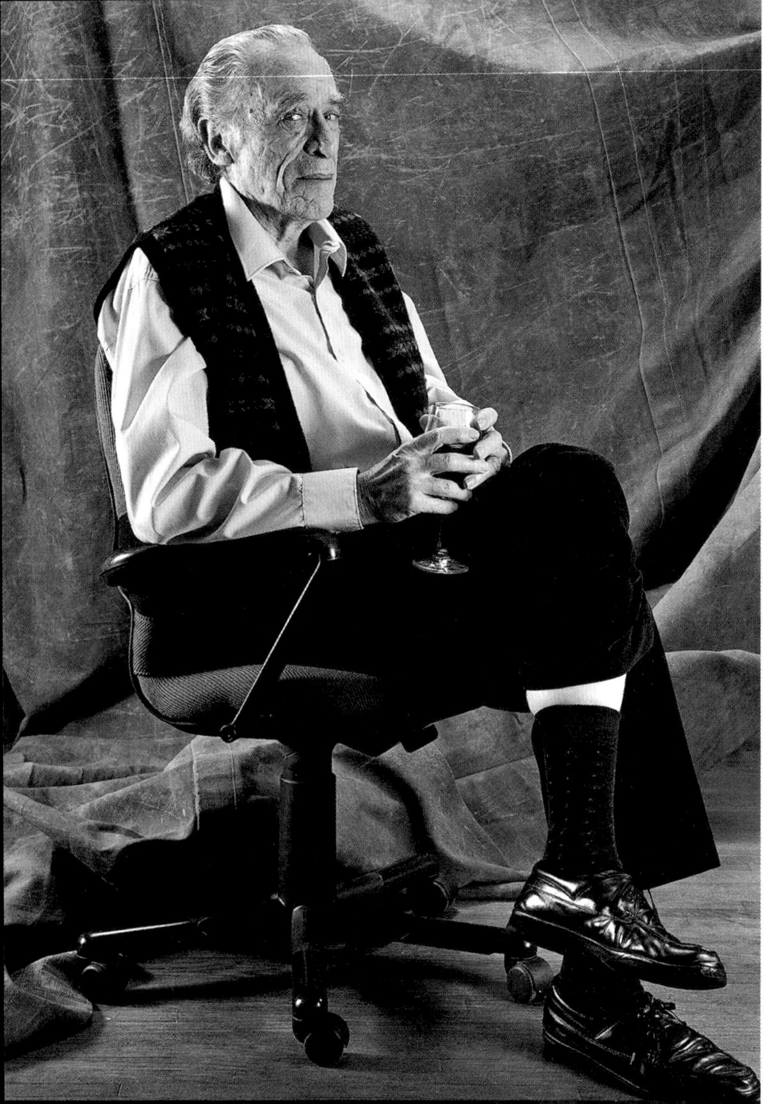

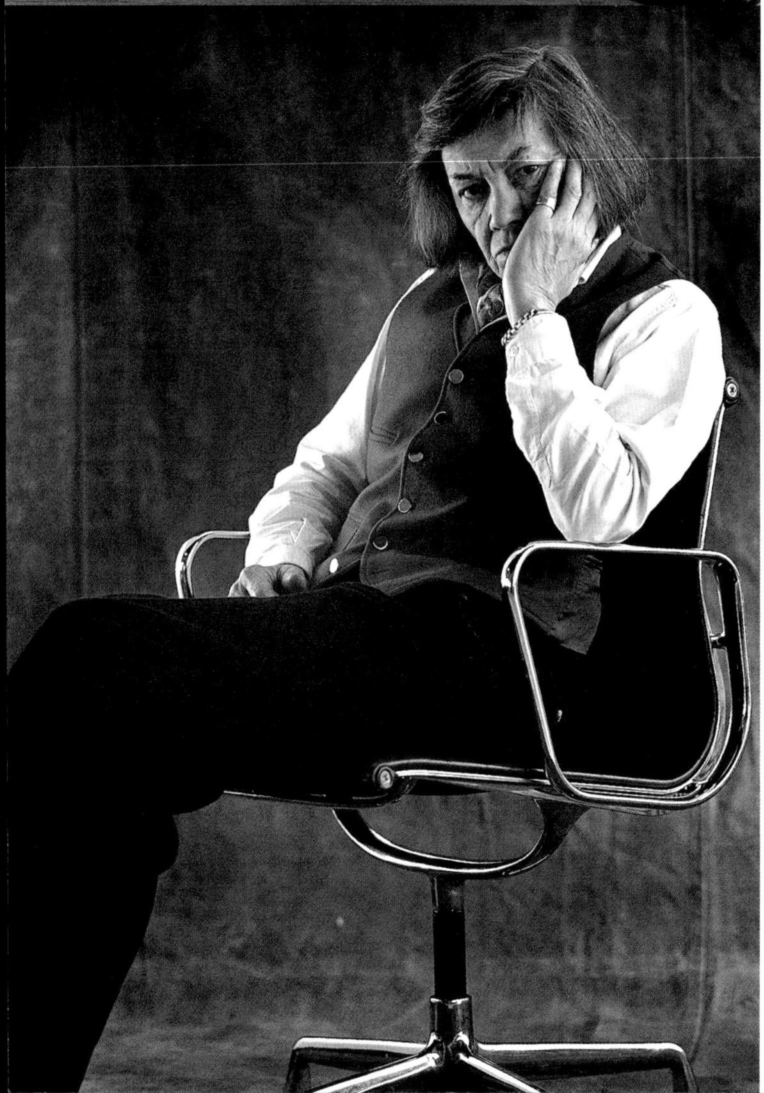

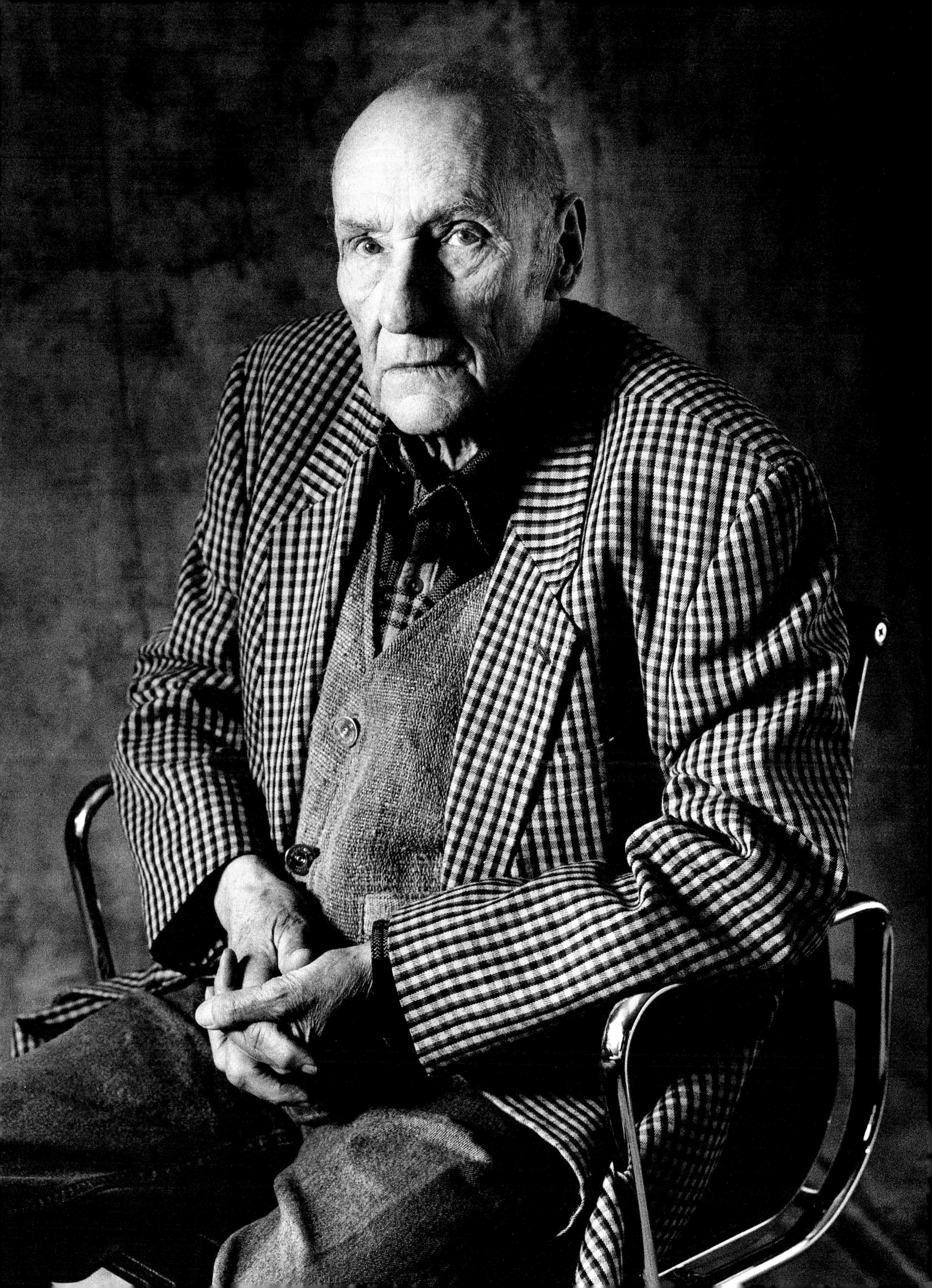

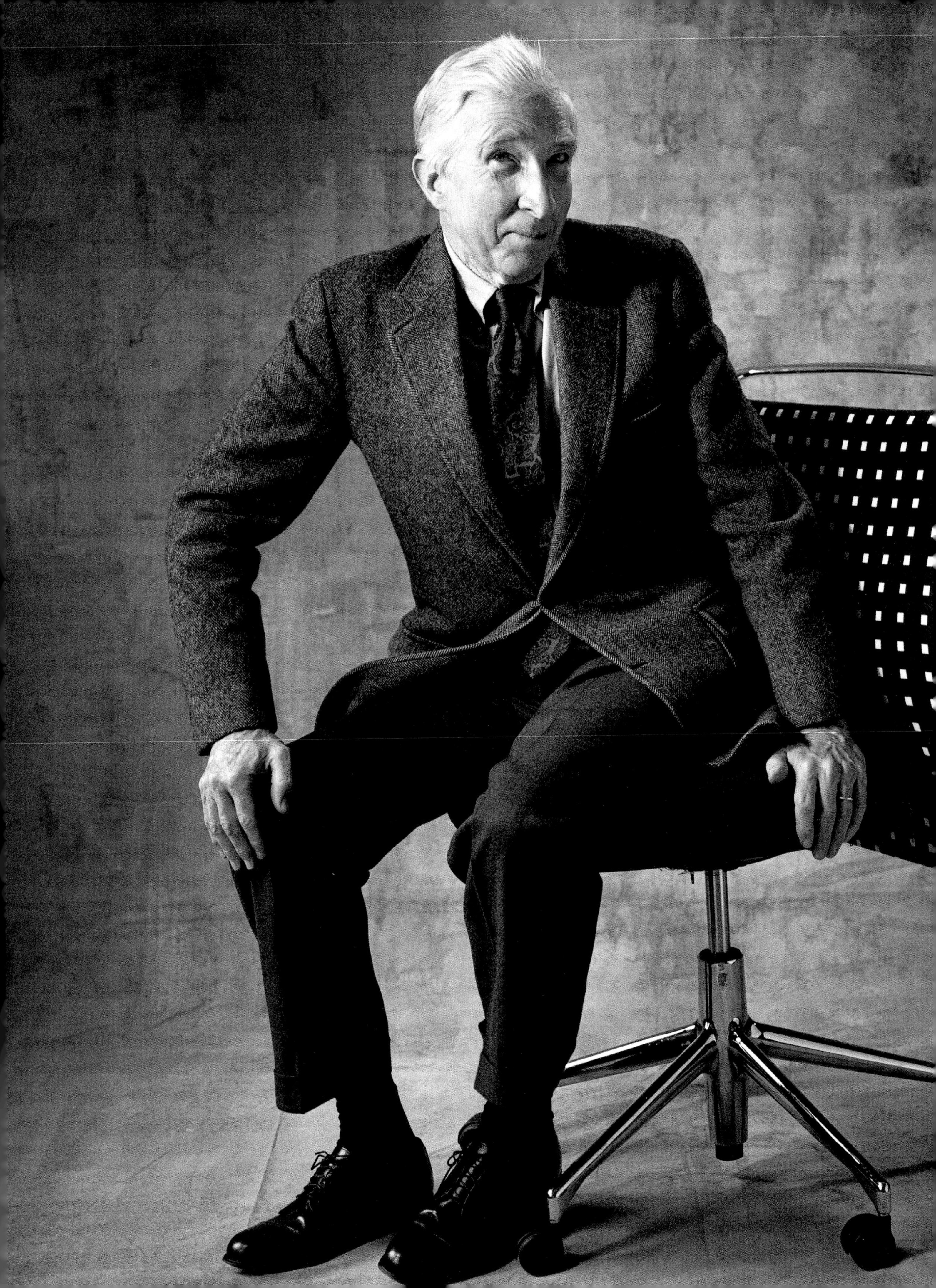

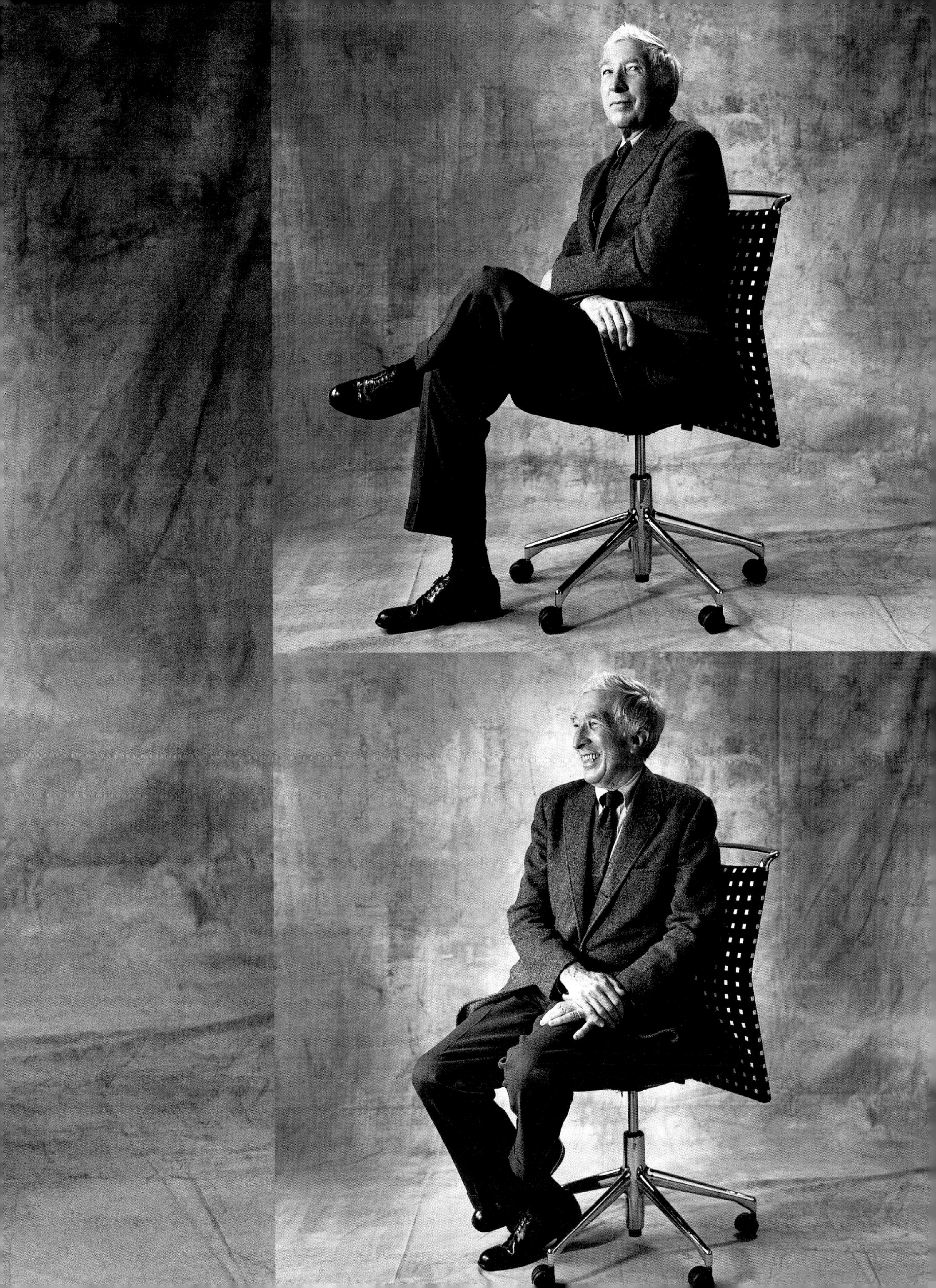

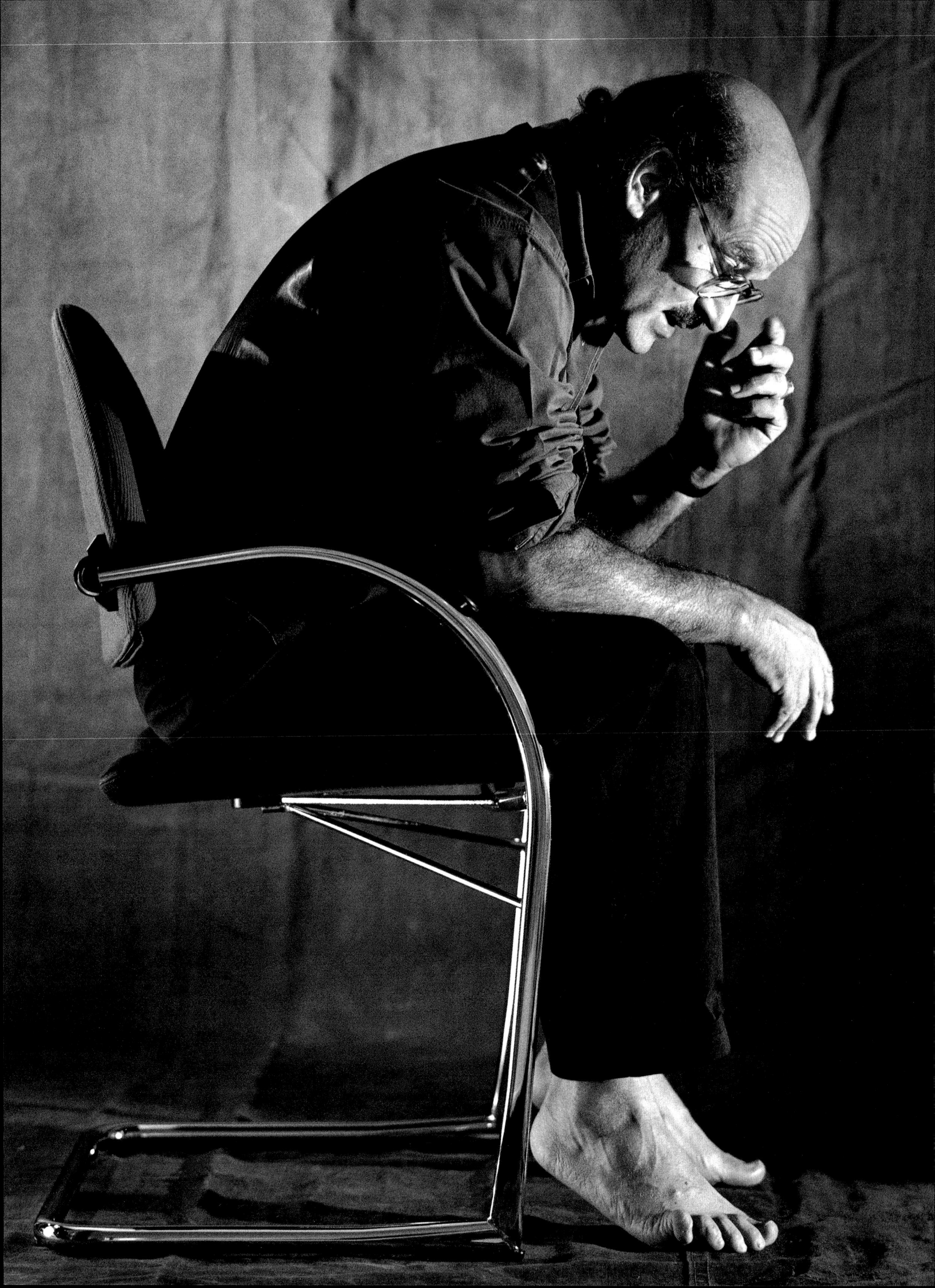

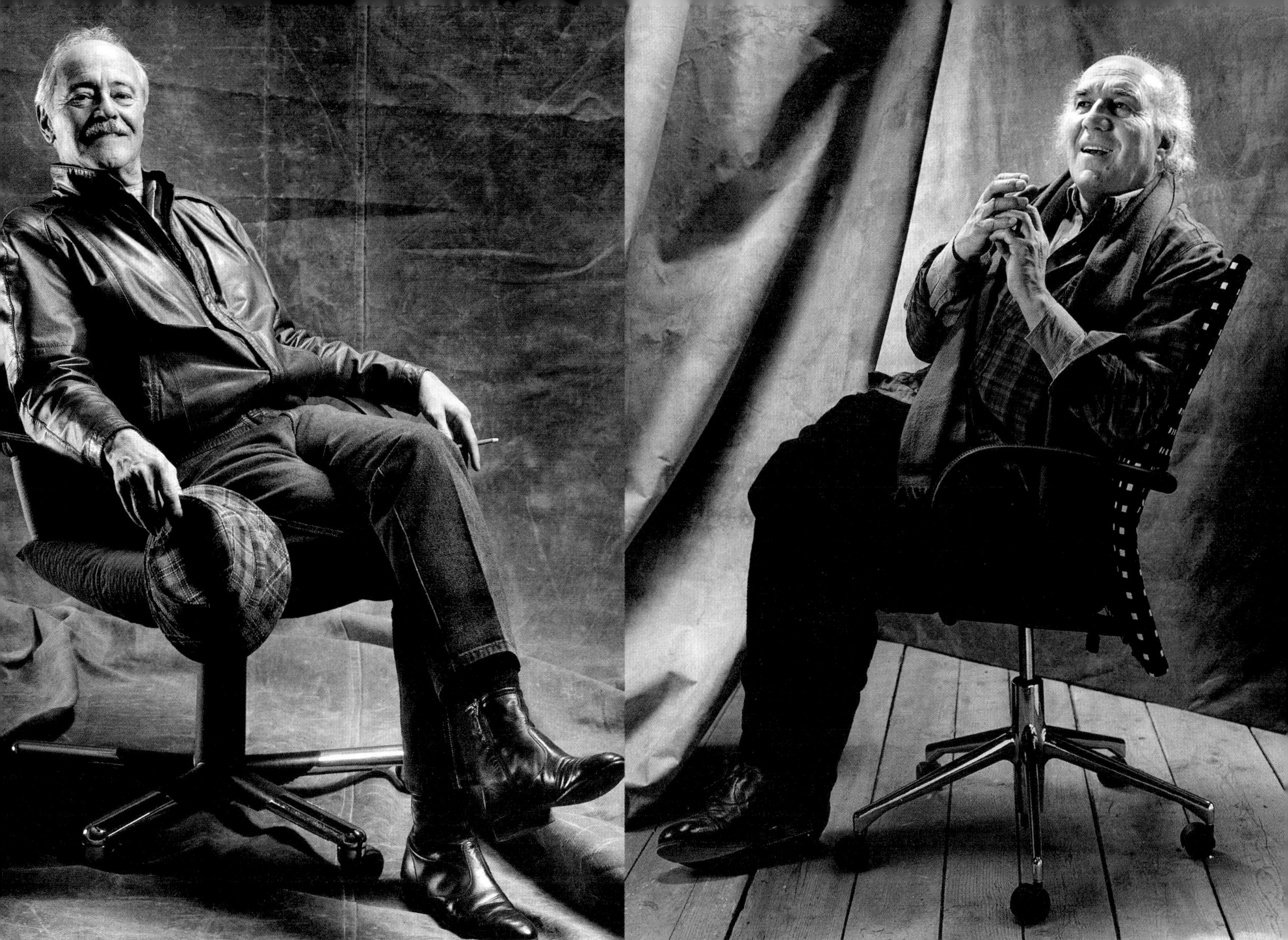

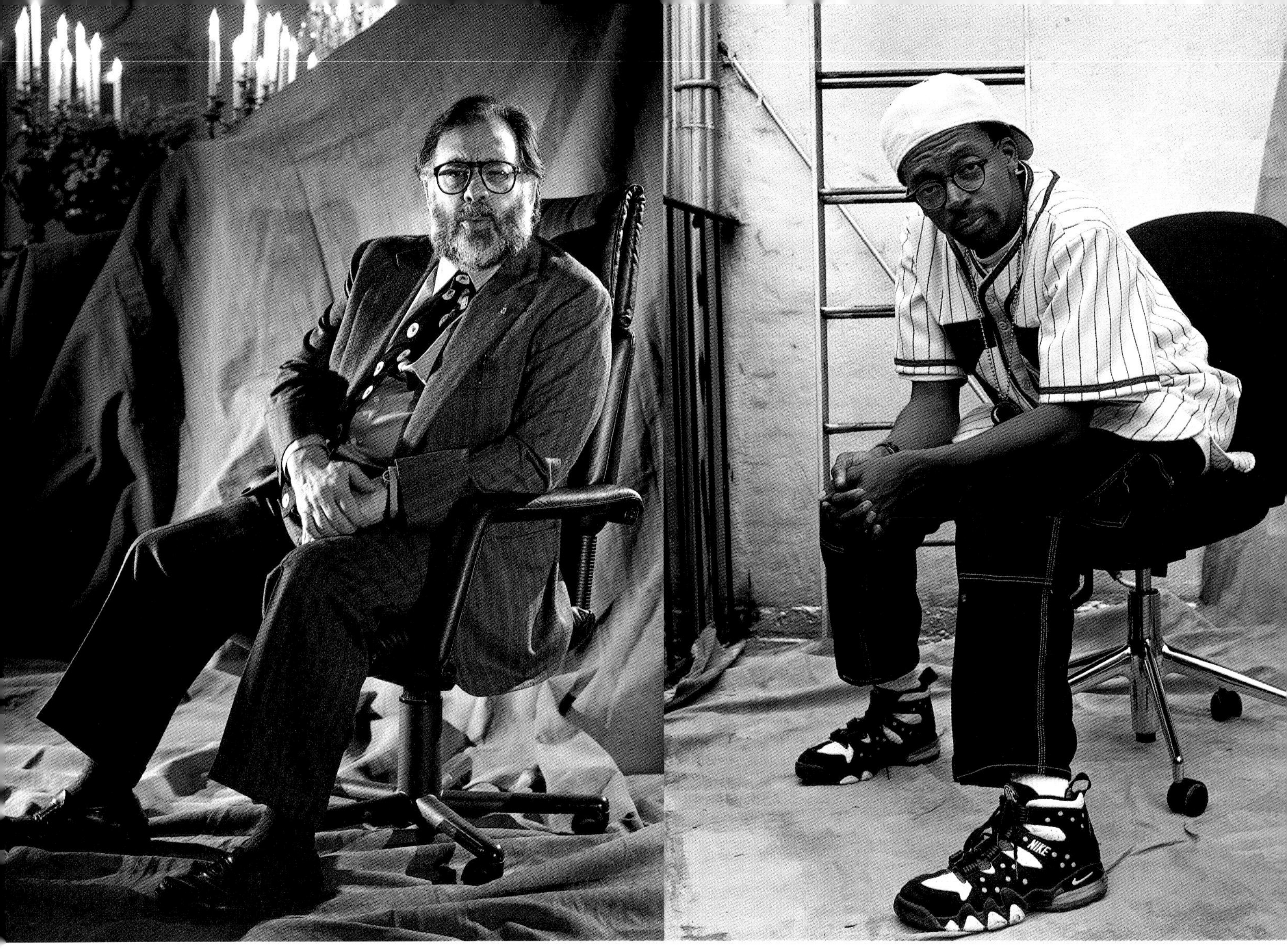
NIKE

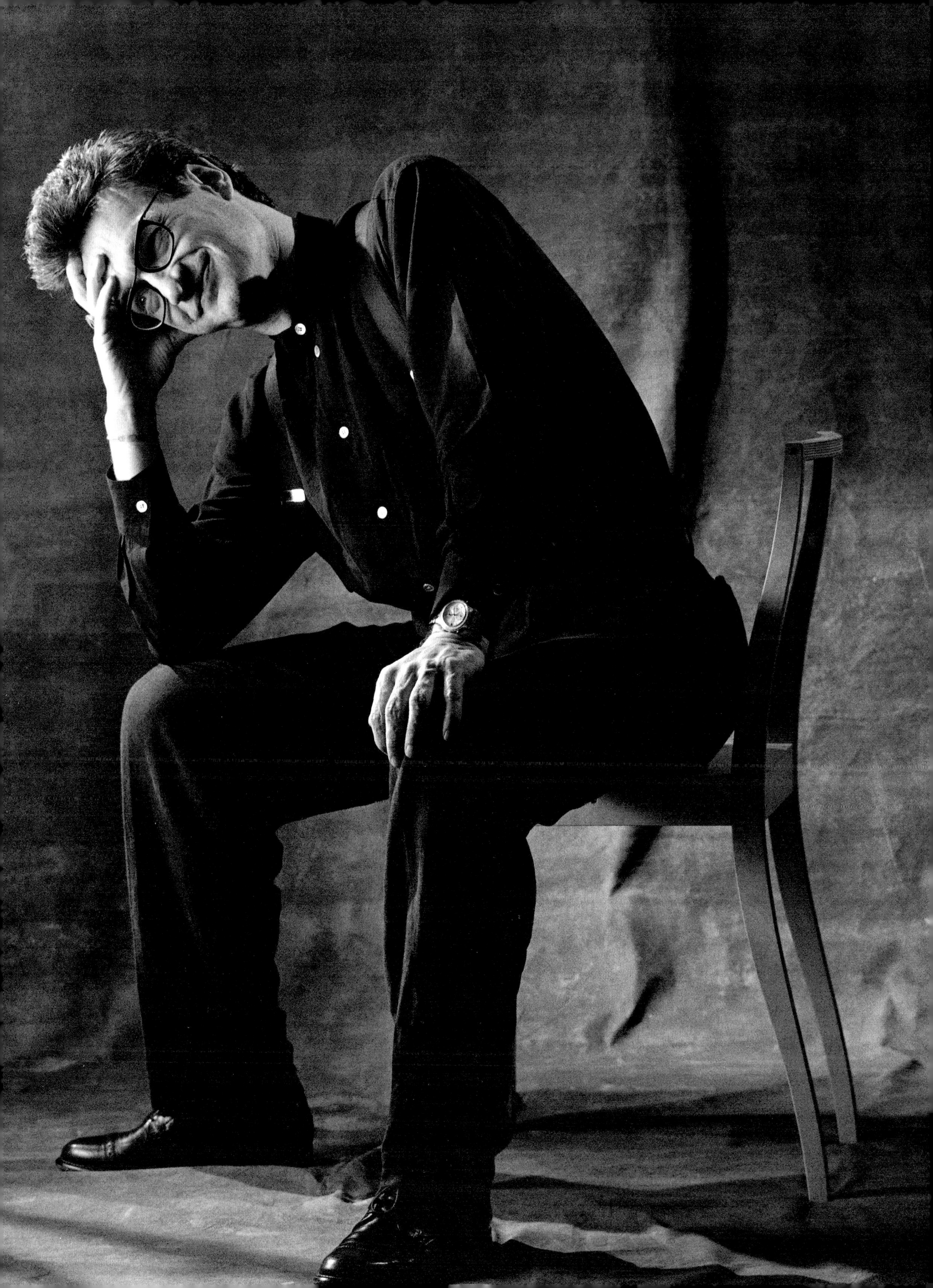

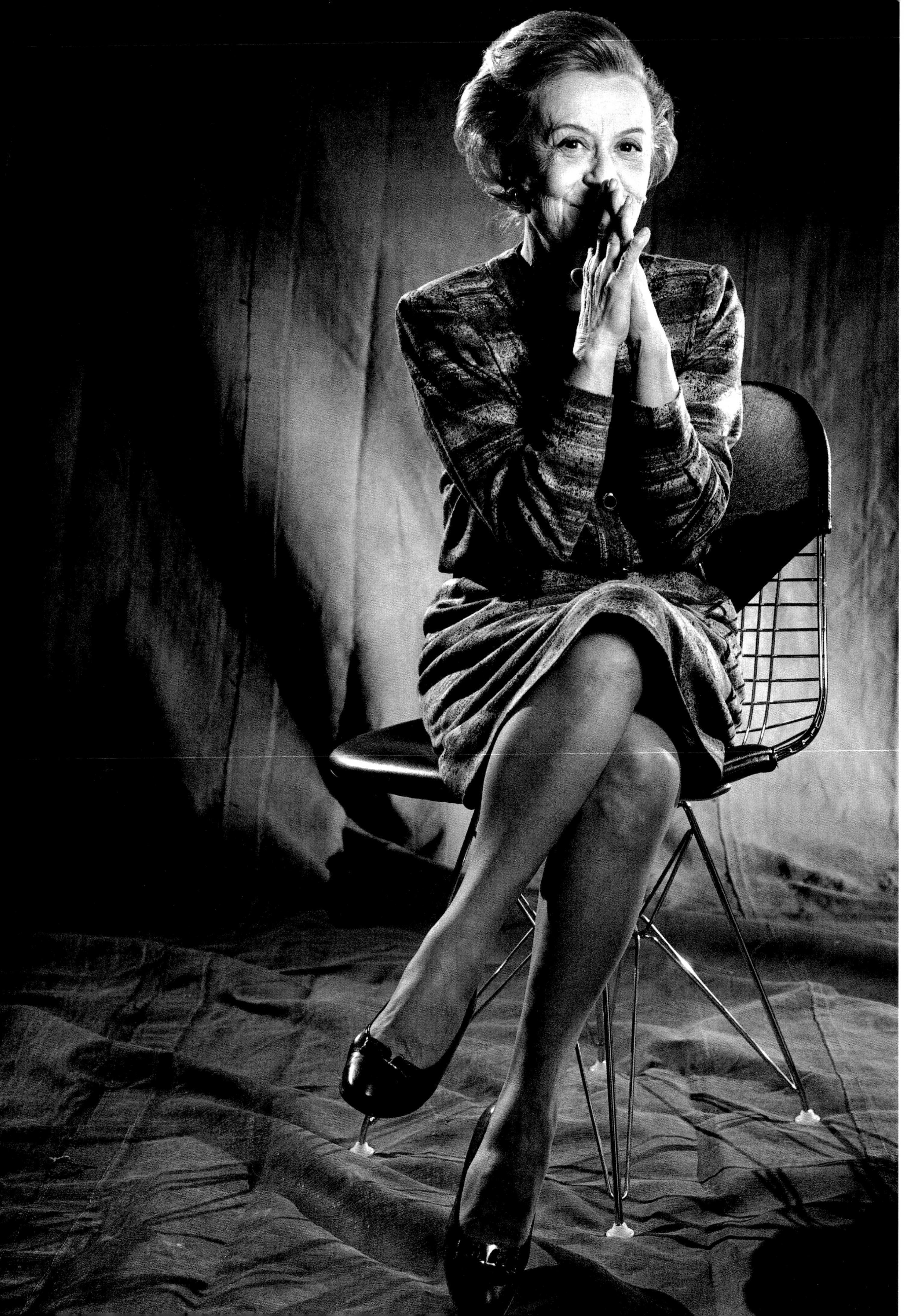

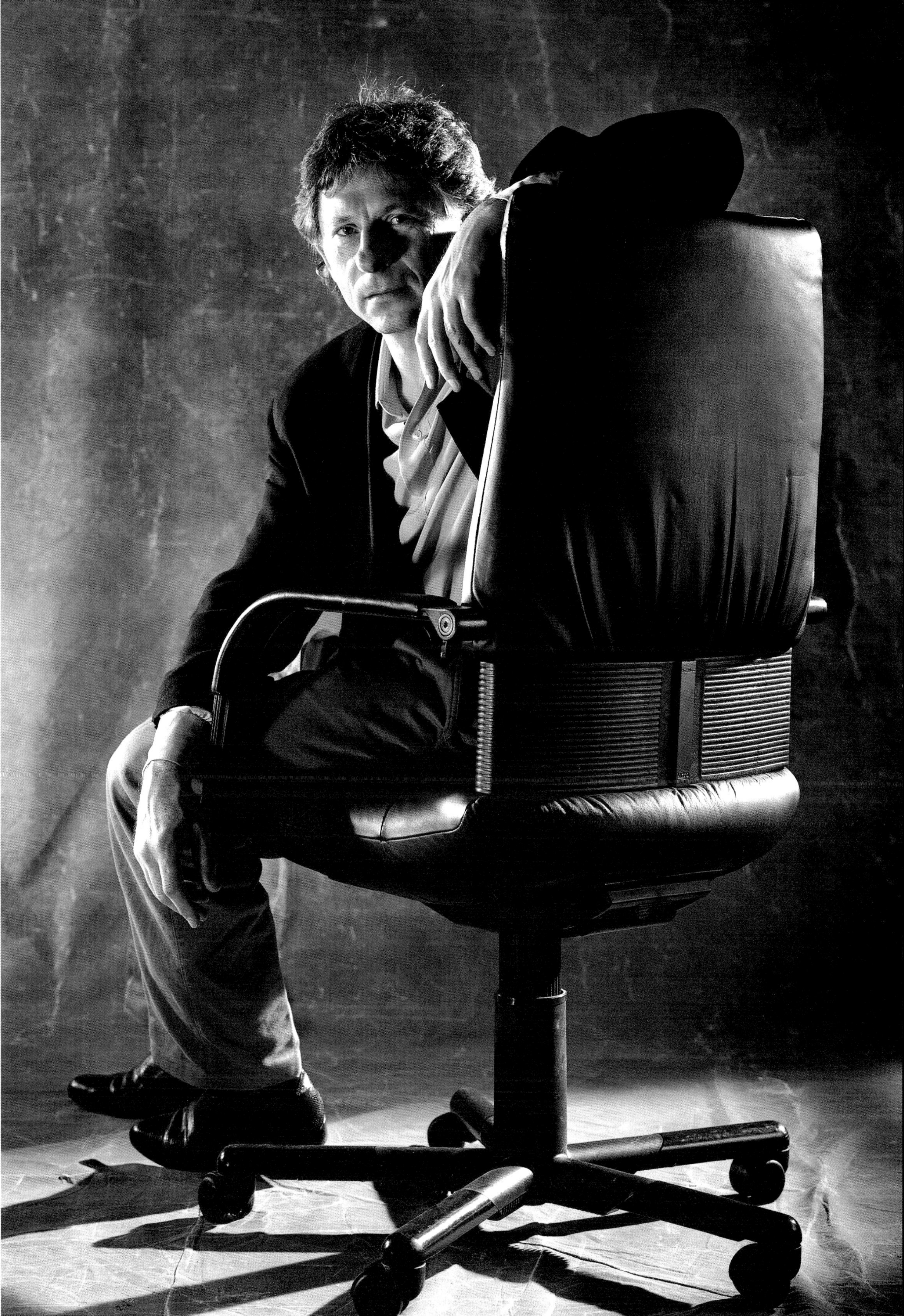

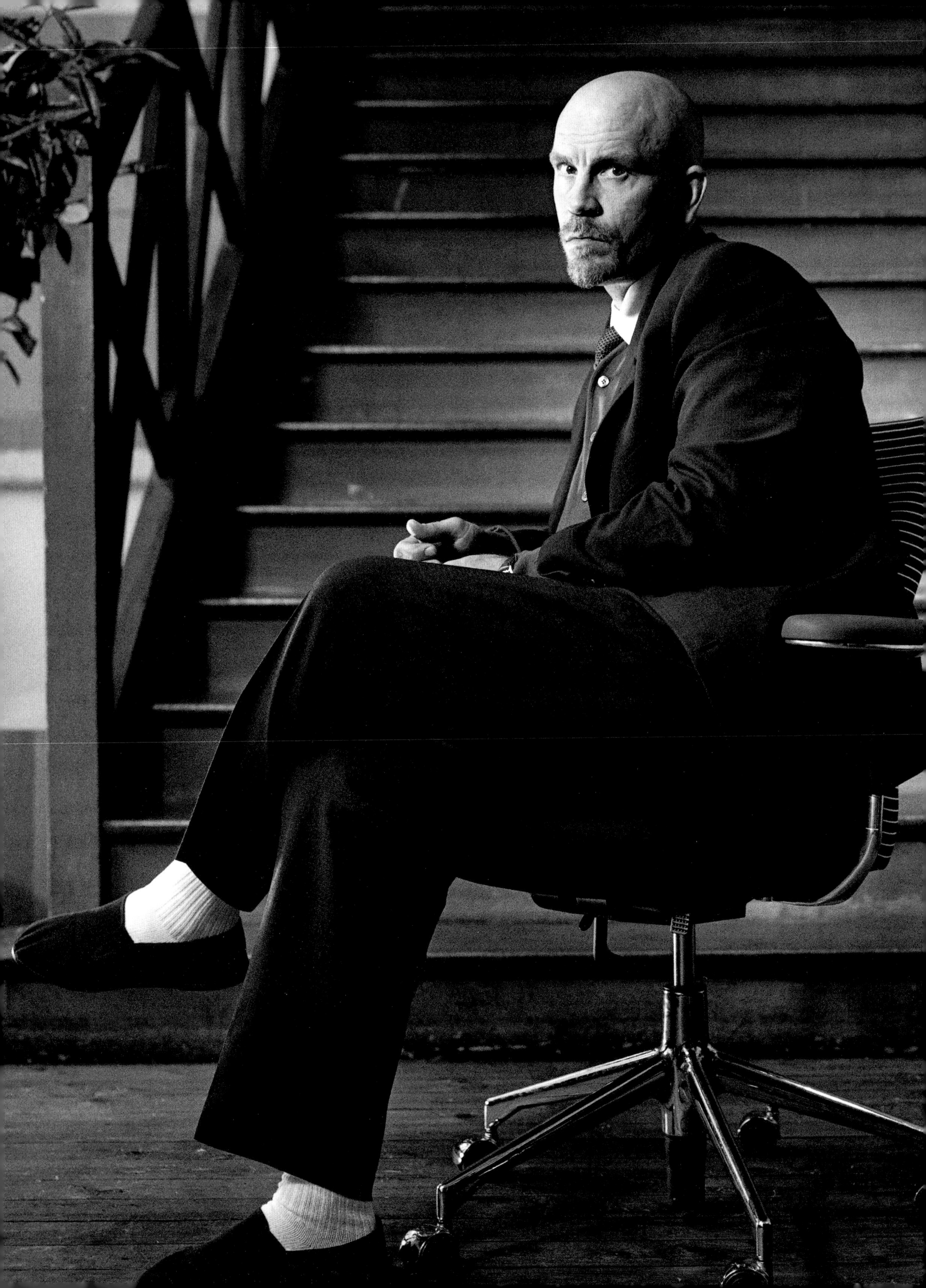

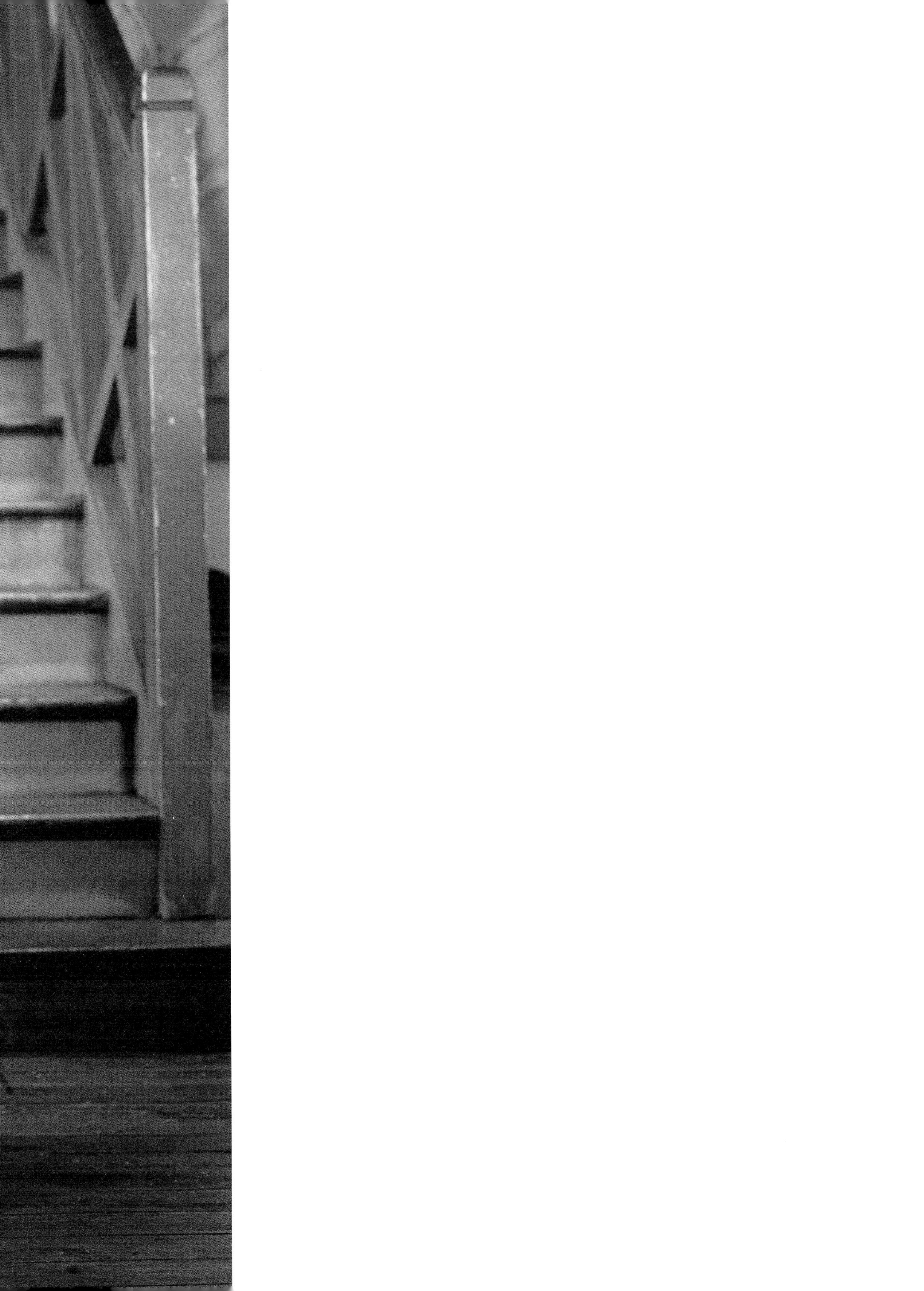

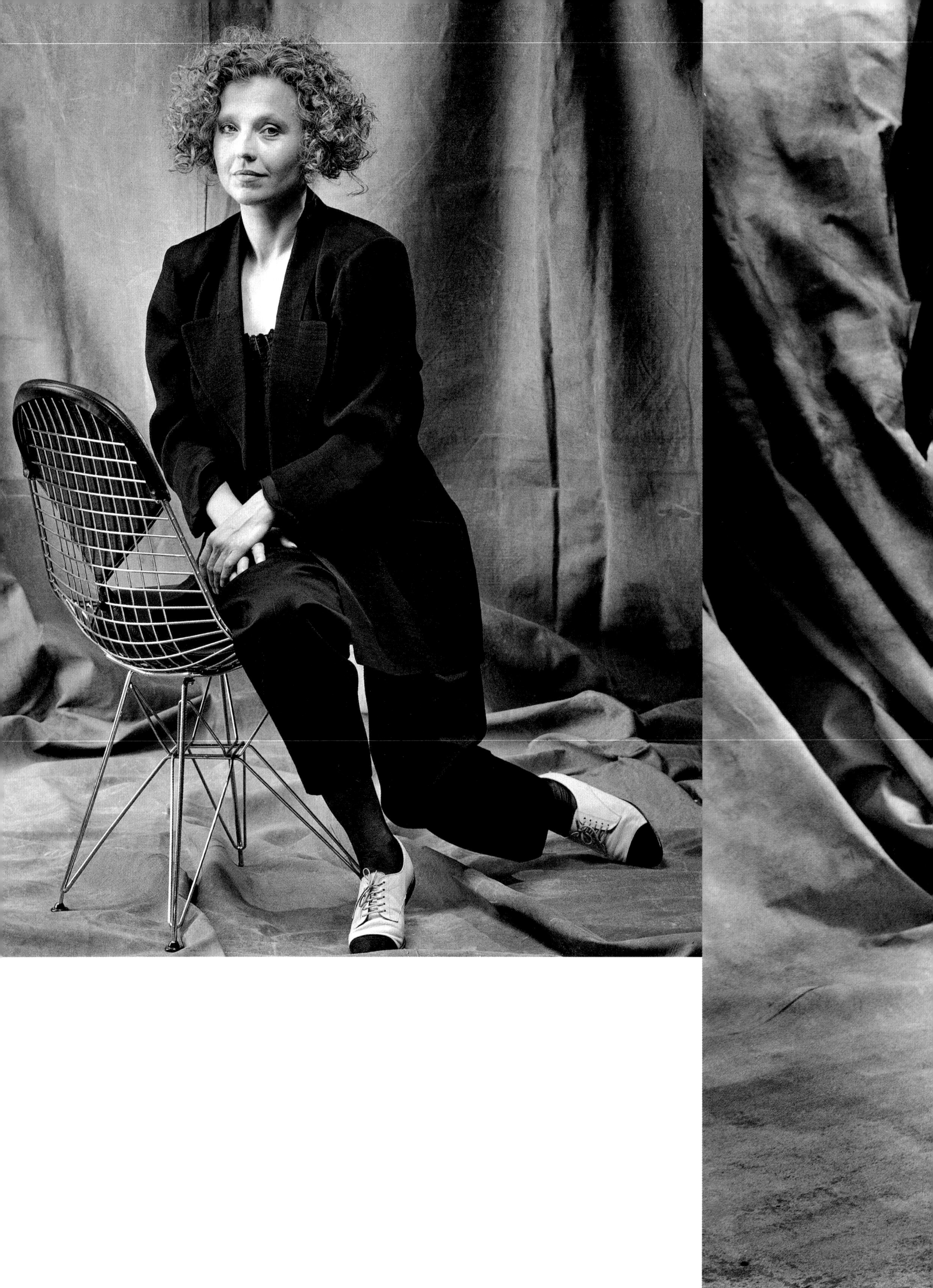

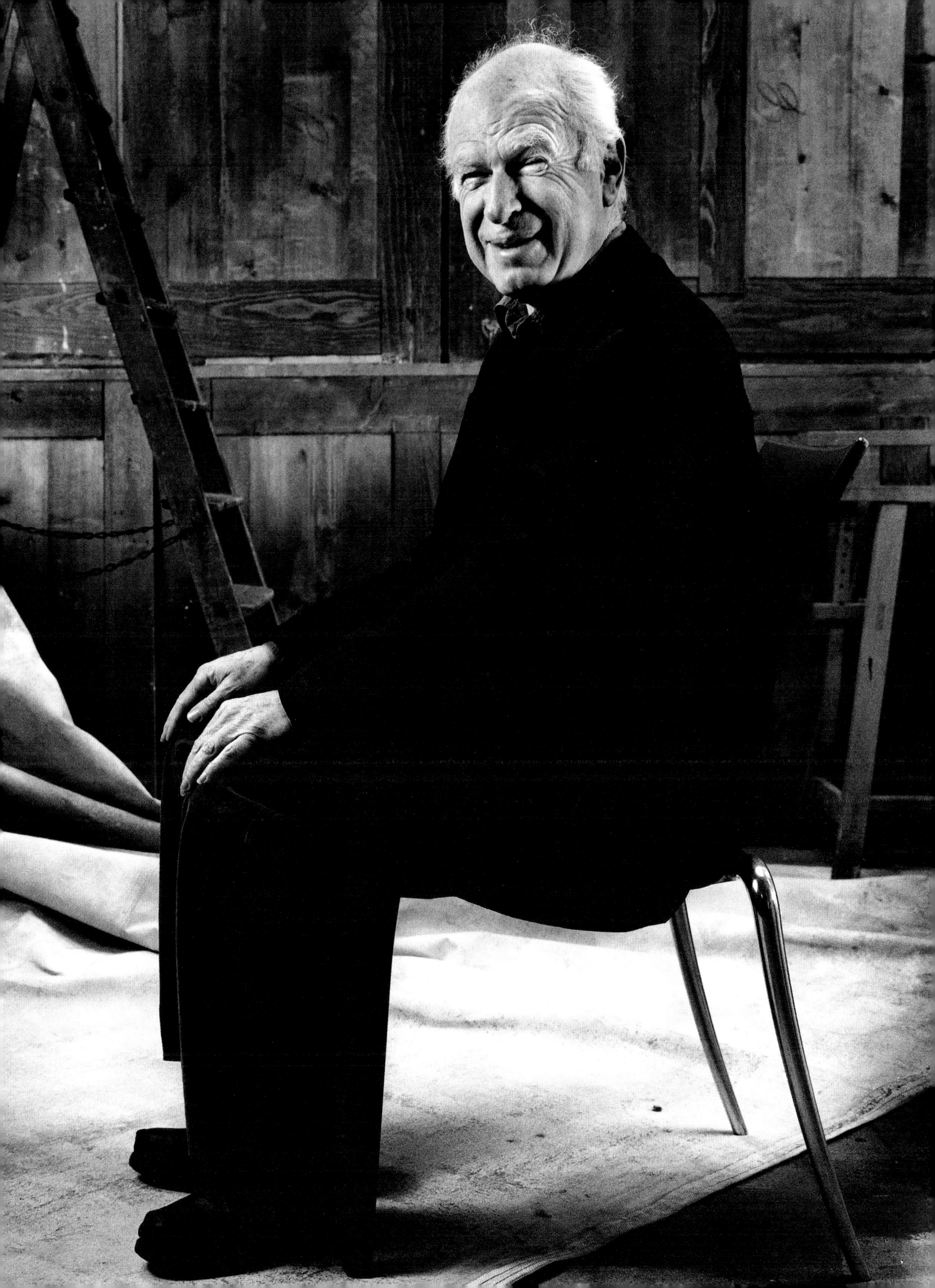

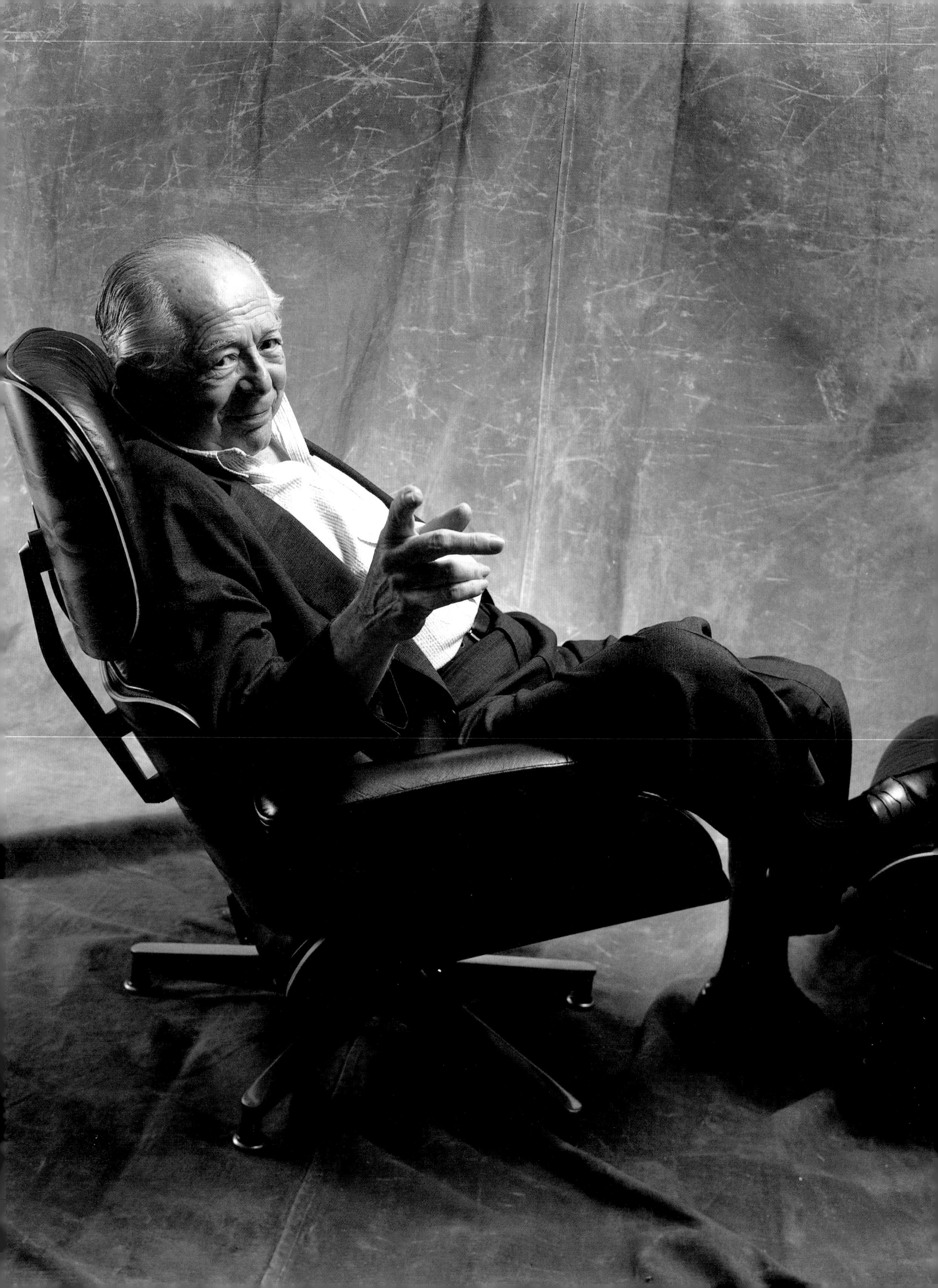

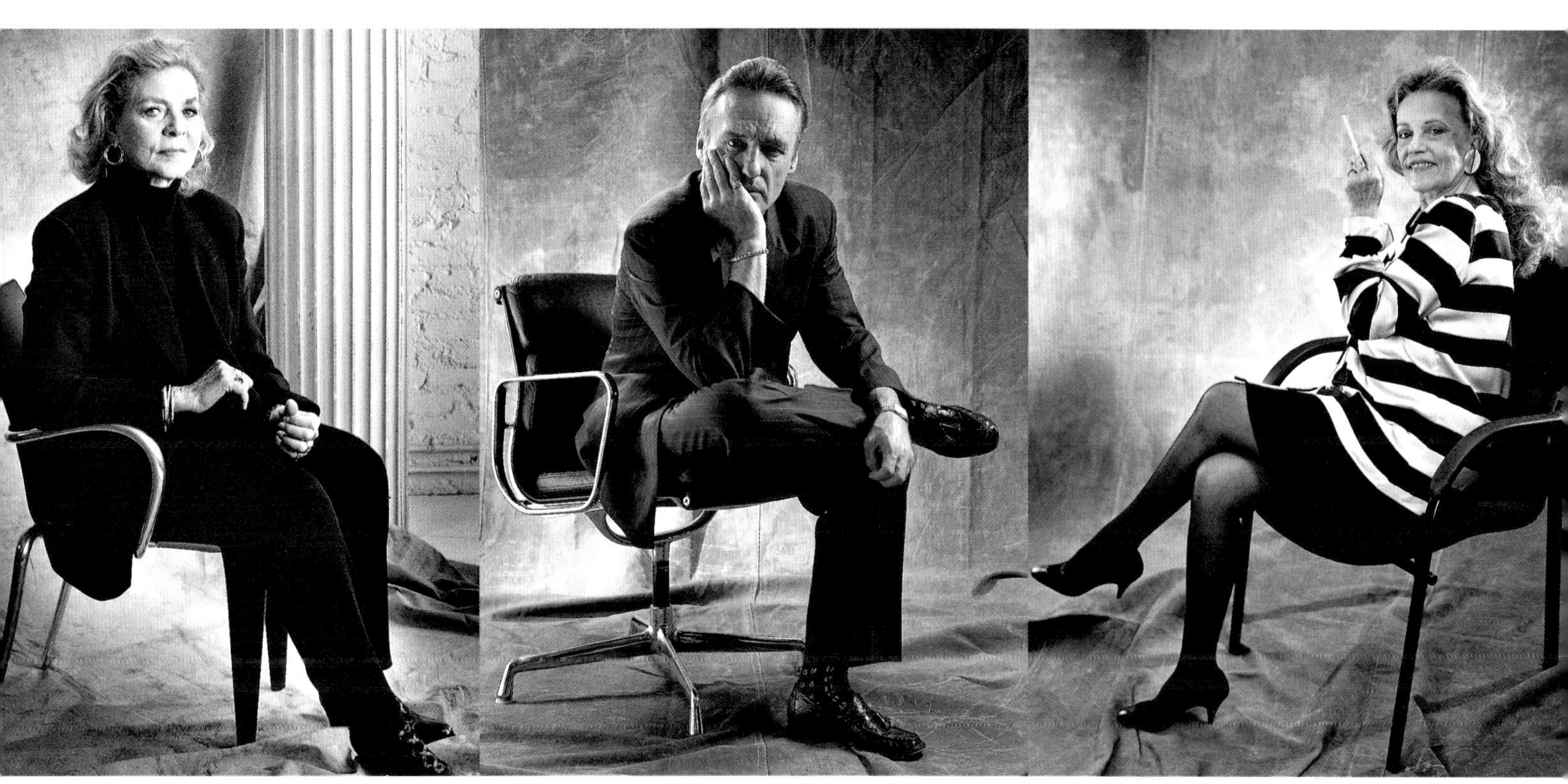

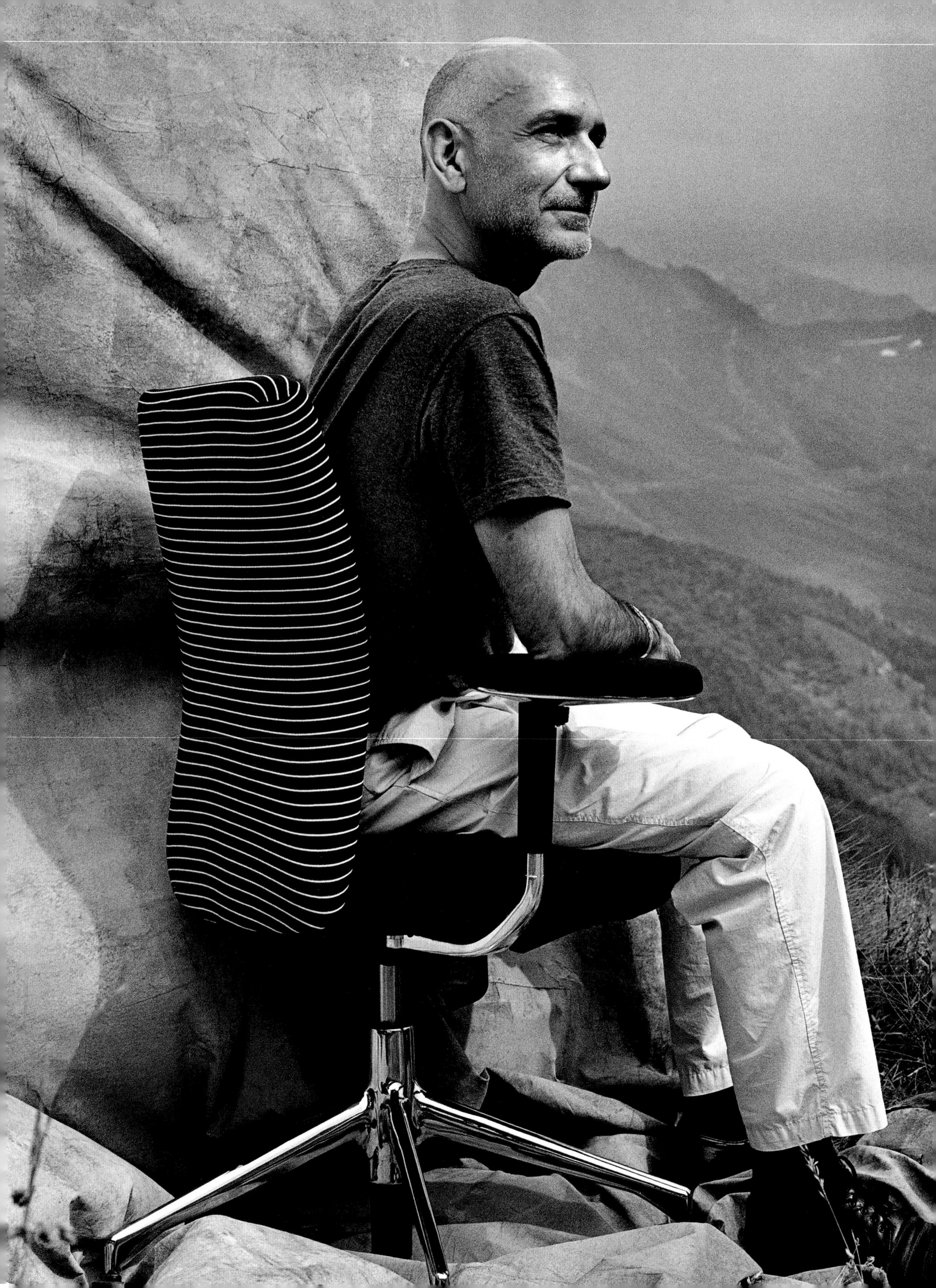

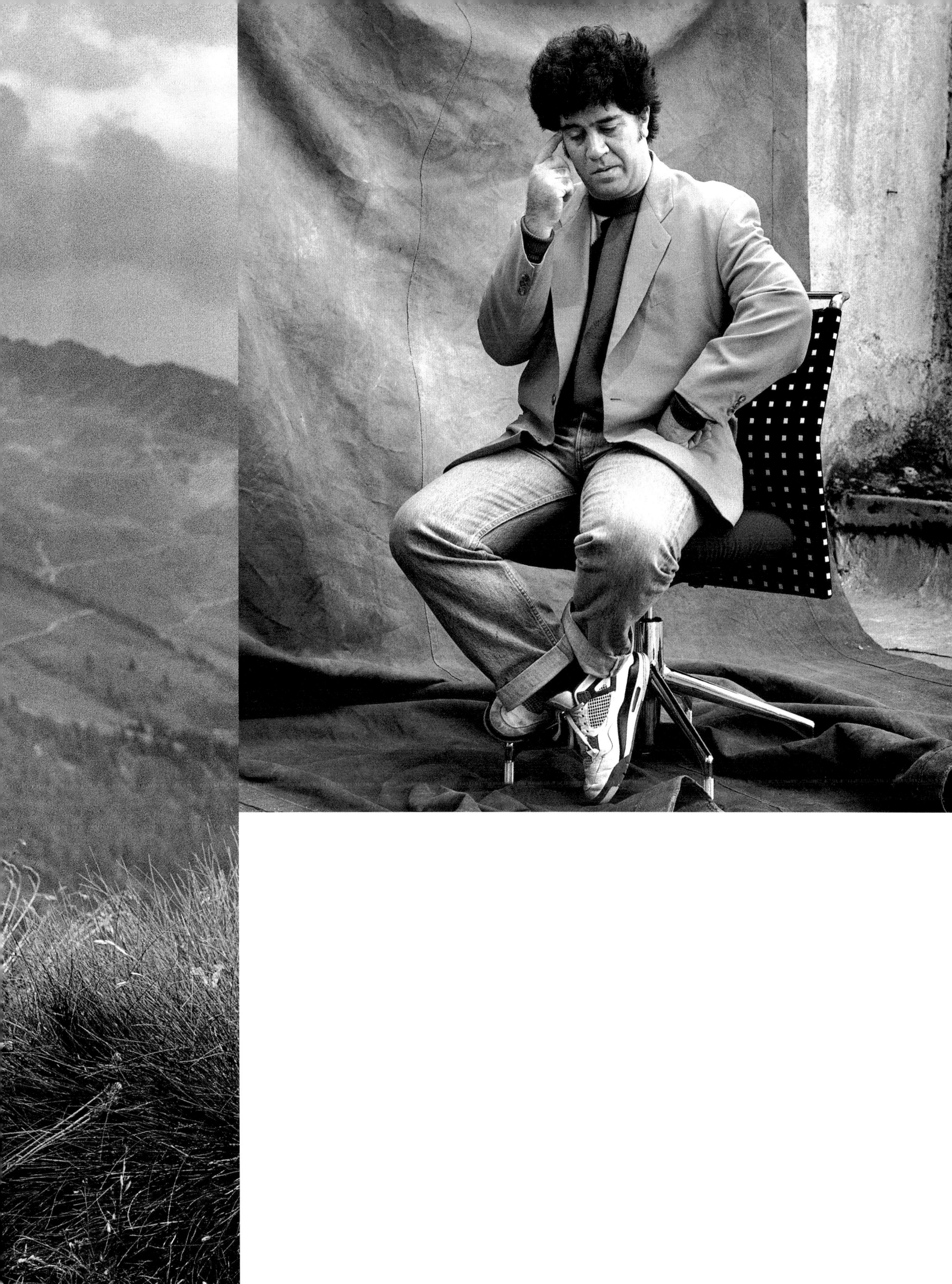

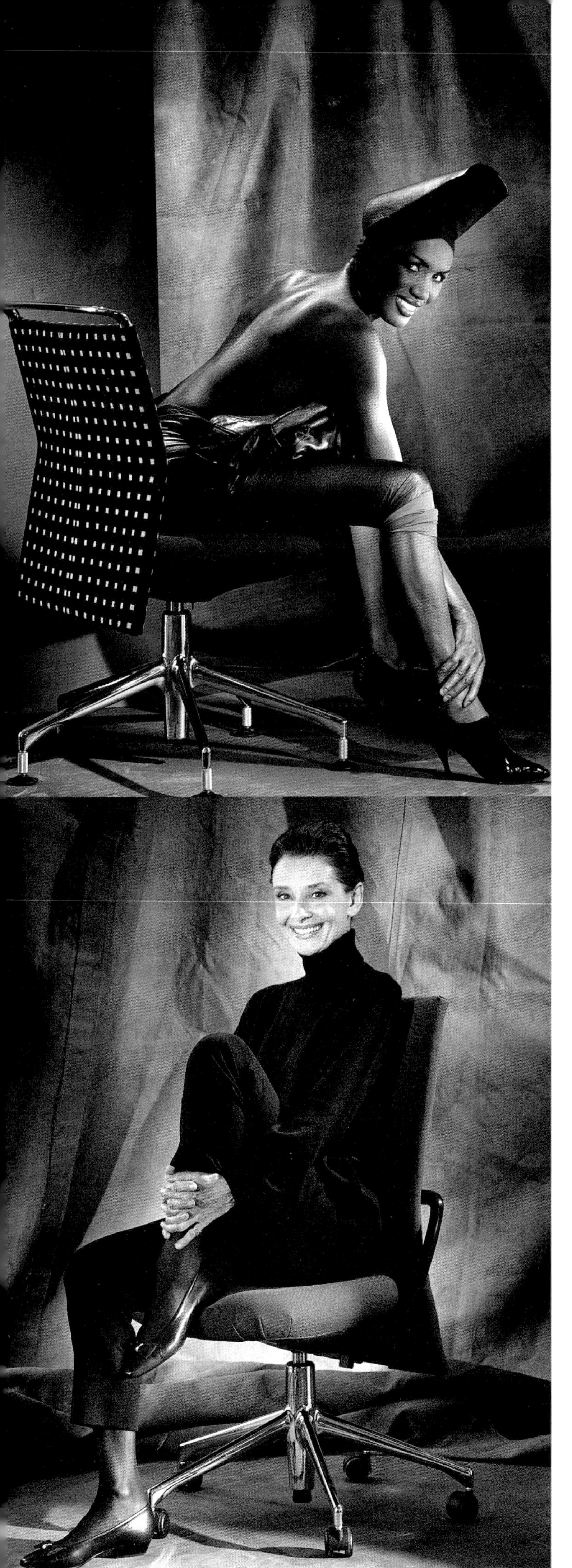

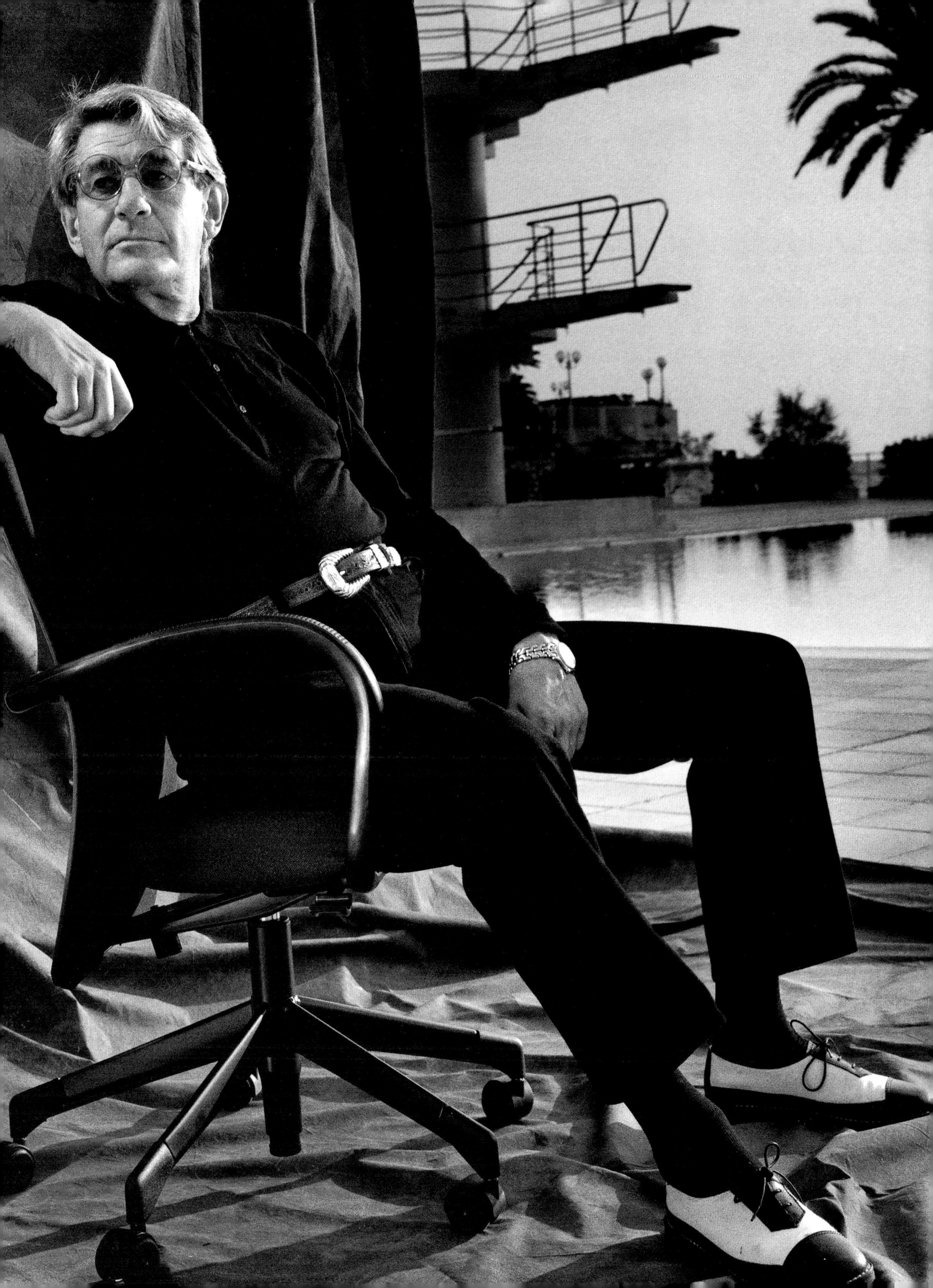

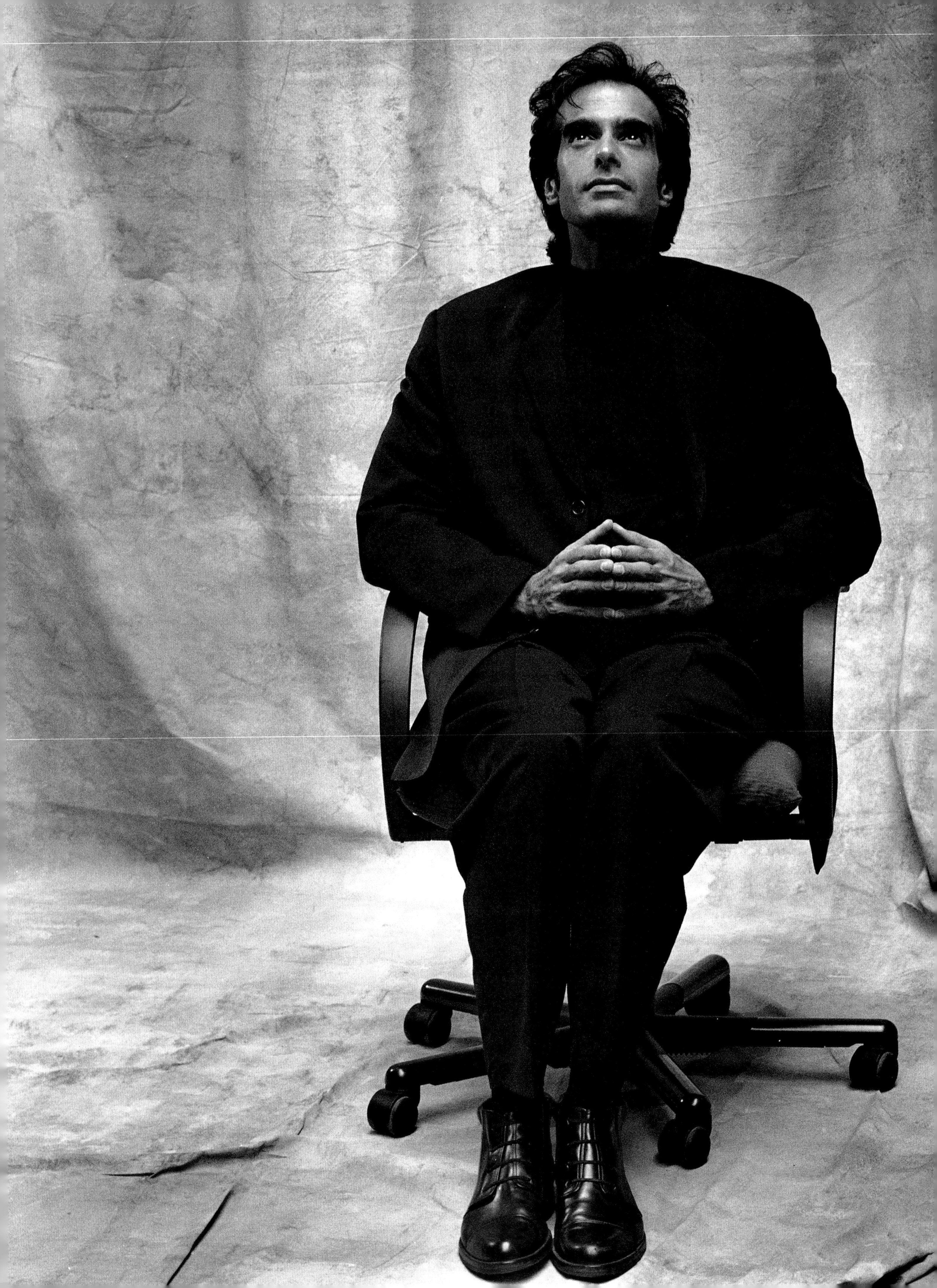

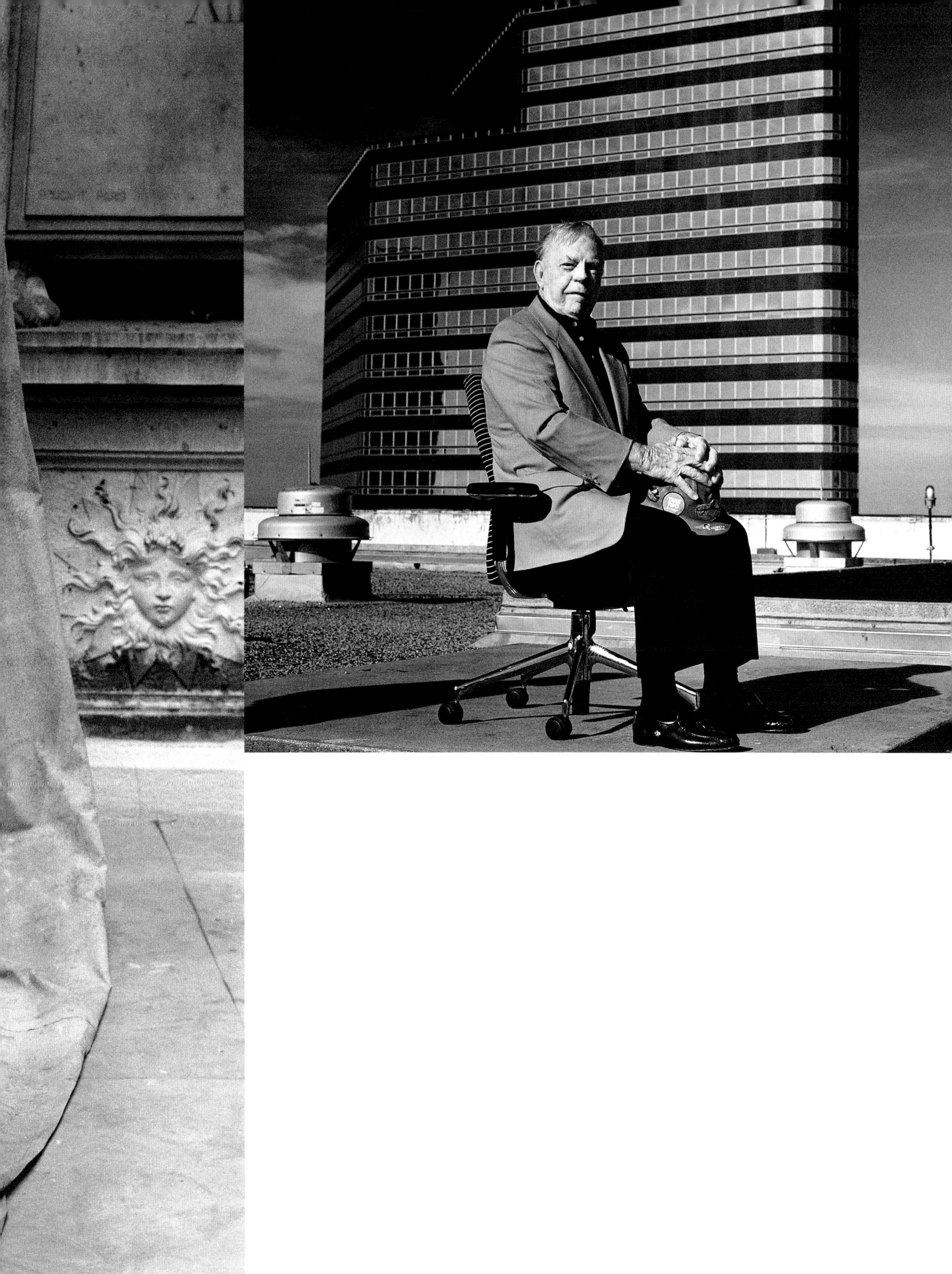

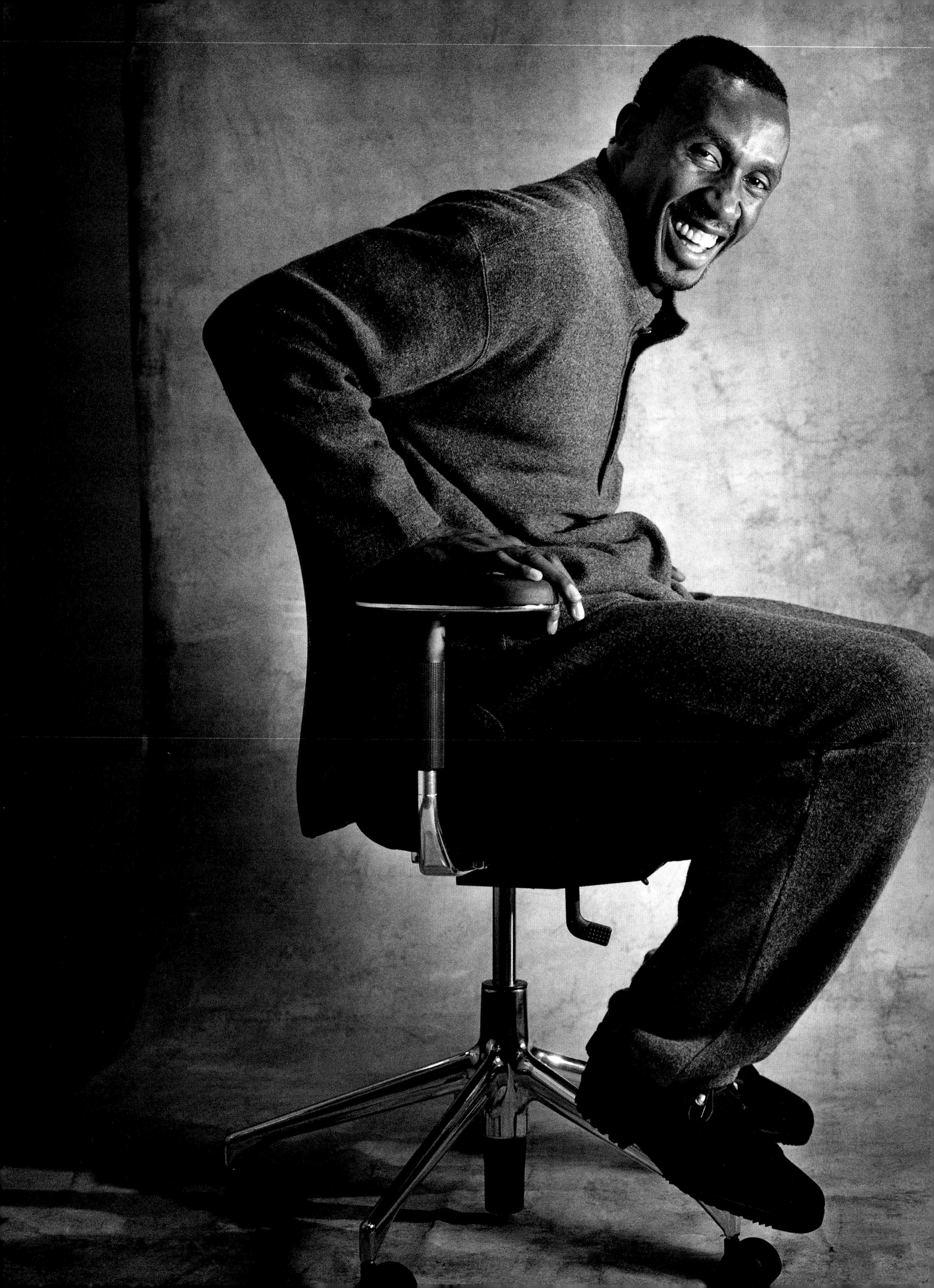

Ray Eames
with great-granddaughter, on Soft Pad Chaise
Design: Charles and Ray Eames

Nigel Kennedy
violonist, on Louis 20
Design: Philippe Starck

Touré Kunda
musicians, on Area
Design: Antonio Citterio with Glen Oliver Löw

Sonny Rollins
musician, on AC 1
Design: Antonio Citterio

Dizzy Gillespie
jazz musician, on Persona
Design: Mario Bellini with Dieter Thiel

Miles Davis
musician, on Onda
Design: Mario Bellini with Dieter Thiel

John Cage
composer, author and artist, on Figura
Design: Mario Bellini with Dieter Thiel

Lou Reed
musician, on Louis 20
Design: Philippe Starck

Laurie Anderson
musician, on Onda
Design: Mario Bellini with Dieter Thiel

Luciano De Crescenzo
author, on Aluminium Chair
Design: Charles and Ray Eames

John Lurie
musician, on Louis 20
Design: Philippe Starck

Cassandra Wilson
jazz singer, on Wire Chair
Design: Charles and Ray Eames

Martin Scorsese
film director, on Aluminium Chair
Design: Charles and Ray Eames

Philip Johnson
architect, on Louis 20
Design: Philippe Starck

Jean Nouvel
architect, on Little Beaver
Design: Frank O. Gehry

Christian de Portzamparc
architect, on Side Chair
Design: Frank Gehry

Ettore Sottsass
architect and designer, on his Teodora (for Vitra Edition)

Frank O. Gehry
architect and designer, on his Little Beaver (for Vitra Edition)

Issey Miyake
fashion designer, on How High The Moon
Design: Shiro Kuramata

Franco Moschino
fashion designer and stylist, on Panton Chair
Design: Verner Panton

Peter Greenaway
film director and author, on Sedlak
Design: Borek Sipek

Frank Stella
artist, on AC 1
Design: Antonio Citterio

Ellsworth Kelly
artist, on Aluminium Chair
Design: Charles and Ray Eames

Tom Wesselmann
artist, on T-Chair
Design: Antonio Citterio with Glen Oliver Löw

Roy Lichtenstein
painter, on Louis 20
Design: Philippe Starck

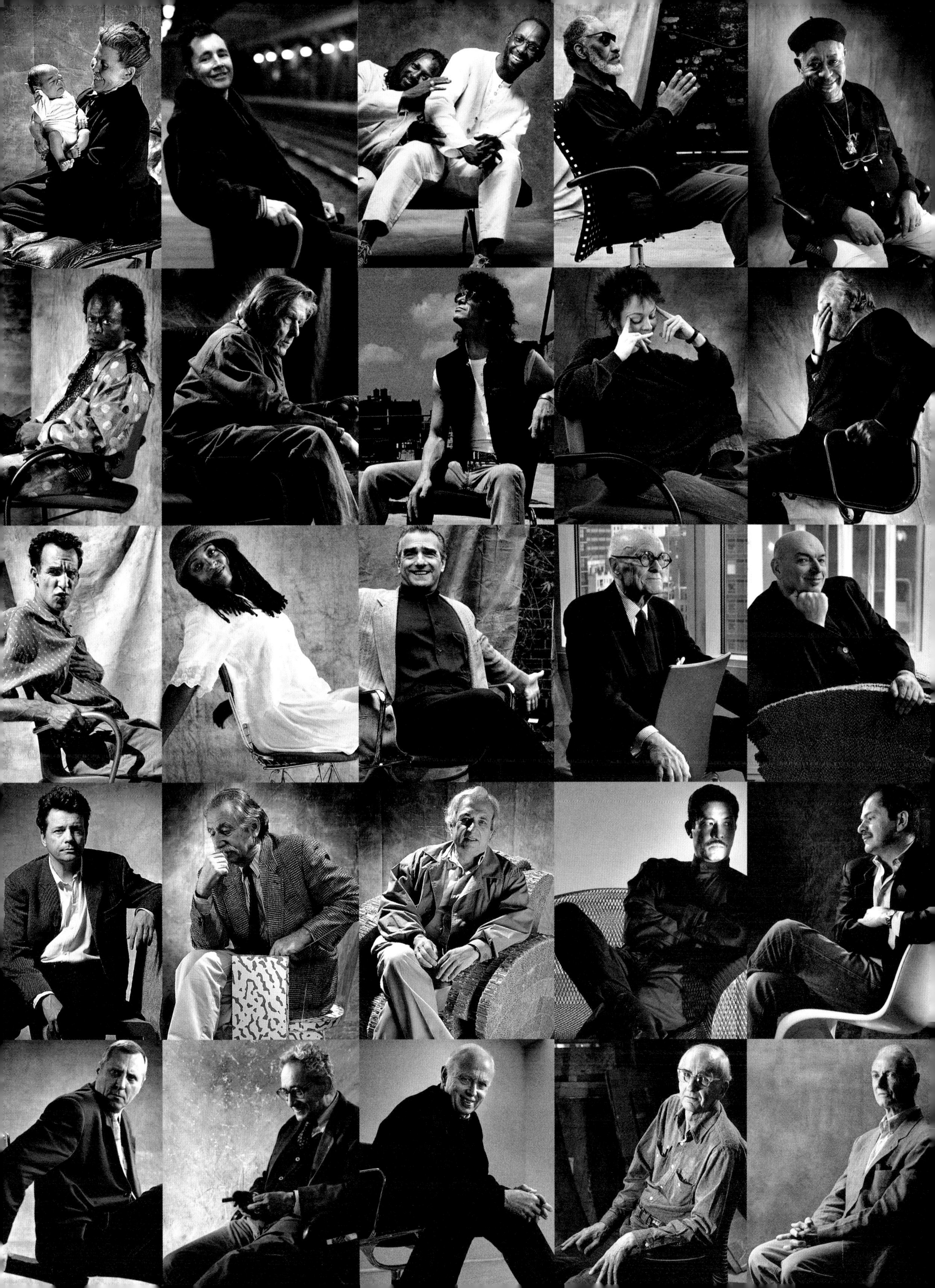

James Rosenquist
artist, on Imago
Design: Mario Bellini with Dieter Thiel

Robert Ryman
artist, on Figura II
Design: Mario Bellini with Dieter Thiel

Robert Wilson
theater director and artist, on Eames Chaise
Design: Charles and Ray Eames

Gilbert and George
artists, on Wire Chairs
Design: Charles and Ray Eames

Keith Haring
artist, on Fiberglass Chair
Design: Charles and Ray Eames

Jeff Koons
artist, on AC 1
Design: Antonio Citterio

Jean Tinguely
artist, on Imago
Design: Mario Bellini with Dieter Thiel

Jörg Immendorff
painter, on Aluminium Chair
Design: Charles and Ray Eames

Jim Dine
artist, on Aluminium Chair
Design: Charles and Ray Eames

Louise Bourgeois
artist, on Louis 20
Design: Philippe Starck

Arnulf Rainer
artist, on Wire Chair
Design: Charles and Ray Eames

Jean-Luc Godard
film director, on Wire Chair
Design: Charles and Ray Eames

Georg Baselitz
artist, on Lounge Chair
Design: Charles and Ray Eames

Jasper Johns
artist, on Ply-Chair
Design: Jasper Morrison

David Hockney
painter, on Persona
Design: Mario Bellini with Dieter Thiel

Merce Cunningham
choreographer, on Ply-Chair
Design: Jasper Morrison

Pina Bausch
ballet director, on Wire Chair
Design: Charles and Ray Eames

Marcia Haydée
prima ballerina and ballet director, on AC 1
Design: Antonio Citterio

Maurice Béjart
choreographer, on Figura
Design: Mario Bellini with Dieter Thiel

Mikhail Baryshnikov
choreographer and ballet dancer, on AC 2
Design: Antonio Citterio

Simon Wiesenthal
Director of the Jewish Documentation Center, on Aluminium Chair
Design: Charles and Ray Eames

Allen Ginsberg
poet, on Visavis
Design: Antonio Citterio

Jean Baudrillard
philosopher, on AC 1
Design: Antonio Citterio

Charles Bukowski
author, on Persona
Design: Mario Bellini with Dieter Thiel

Patricia Highsmith
author, on Aluminium Chair
Design: Charles and Ray Eames

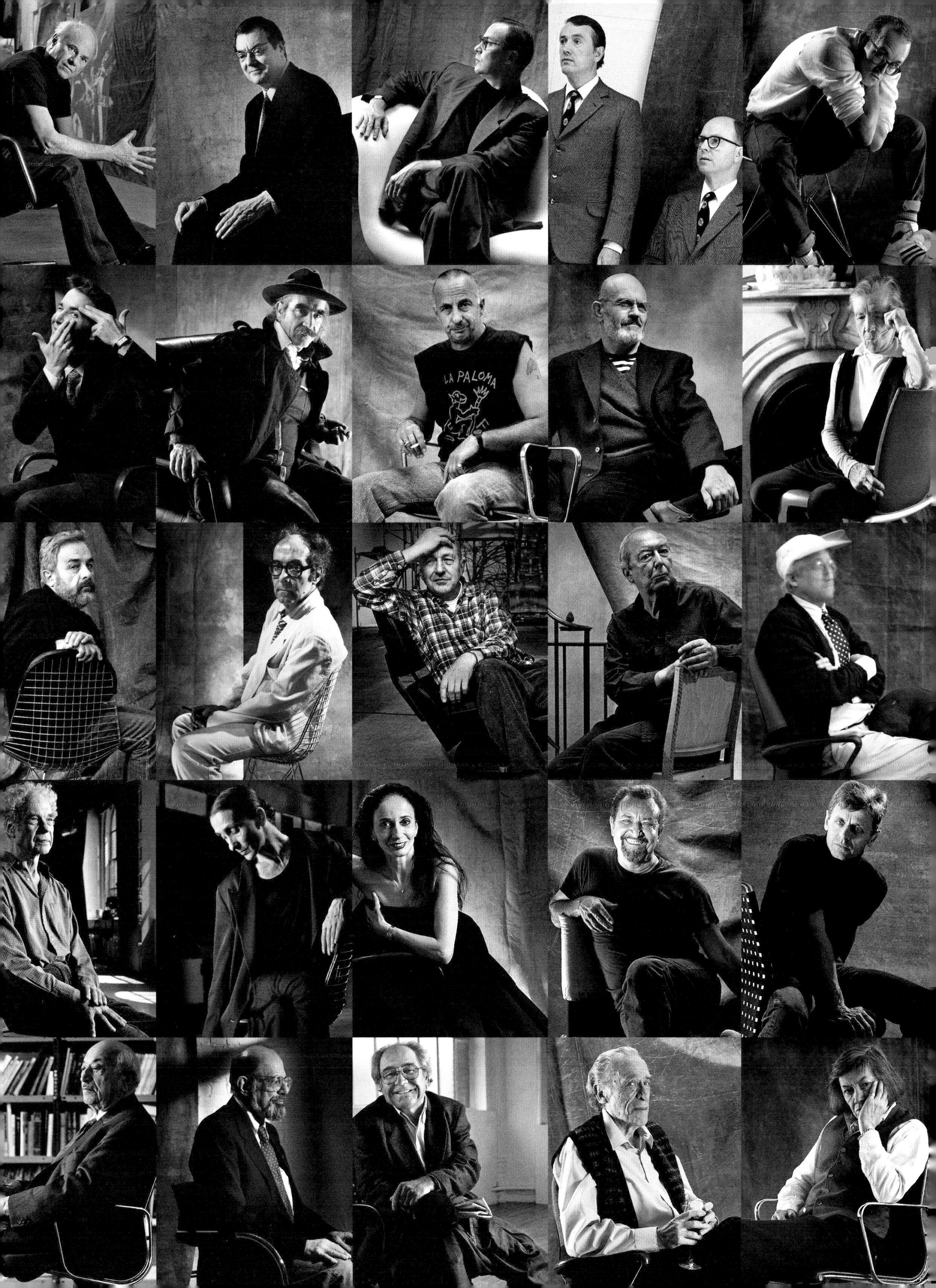
LA PALOMA

William Burroughs
writer, on Aluminium Chair
Design: Charles and Ray Eames

John Updike
author, on AC 2
Design: Antonio Citterio

Volker Schlöndorff
film director, on Onda
Design: Mario Bellini with Dieter Thiel

Jack Lemmon
actor, on Figura
Design: Mario Bellini with Dieter Thiel

Michel Piccoli
actor, on AC 1
Design: Antonio Citterio

Francis Ford Coppola
film director and producer, on Imago
Design: Mario Bellini with Dieter Thiel

Spike Lee
film director, on Axion
Design: Antonio Citterio with Glen Oliver Löw

Wim Wenders
film director, on Ply-Chair
Design: Jasper Morrison

Giuletta Masina
actress, on Wire Chair
Design: Charles and Ray Eames

Roman Polanski
film director, on Figura
Design: Mario Bellini with Dieter Thiel

John Malkovich
actor, on T-Chair
Design: Antonio Citterio with Glen Oliver Löw

Hanna Schygulla
actress, on Wire Chair
Design: Charles and Ray Eames

Peter Brook
theater director, on Louis 20
Design: Philippe Starck

Billy Wilder
film director, on Lounge Chair
Design: Charles and Ray Eames

Lauren Bacall
actress, on Louis 20
Design: Philippe Starck

Dennis Hopper
actor, on Soft Pad Chair
Design: Charles and Ray Eames

Jeanne Moreau
actress, on Persona
Design: Mario Bellini with Dieter Thiel

Ben Kingsley
actor, on T-Chair
Design: Antonio Citterio with Glen Oliver Löw

Pedro Almodóvar
film director, on AC 2
Design: Antonio Citterio

Grace Jones
actress and singer, on AC 2
Design: Antonio Citterio

Audrey Hepburn
actress and UNICEF ambassador, on AC 1
Design: Antonio Citterio

Helmut Newton
photographer, on AC 1
Design: Antonio Citterio

David Copperfield
magician, on Figura II
Design: Mario Bellini with Dieter Thiel

Red Adair
firefighter, on T-Chair
Design: Antonio Citterio

Linford Christie
sprinter, on T-Chair
Design: Antonio Citterio with Glen Oliver Löw

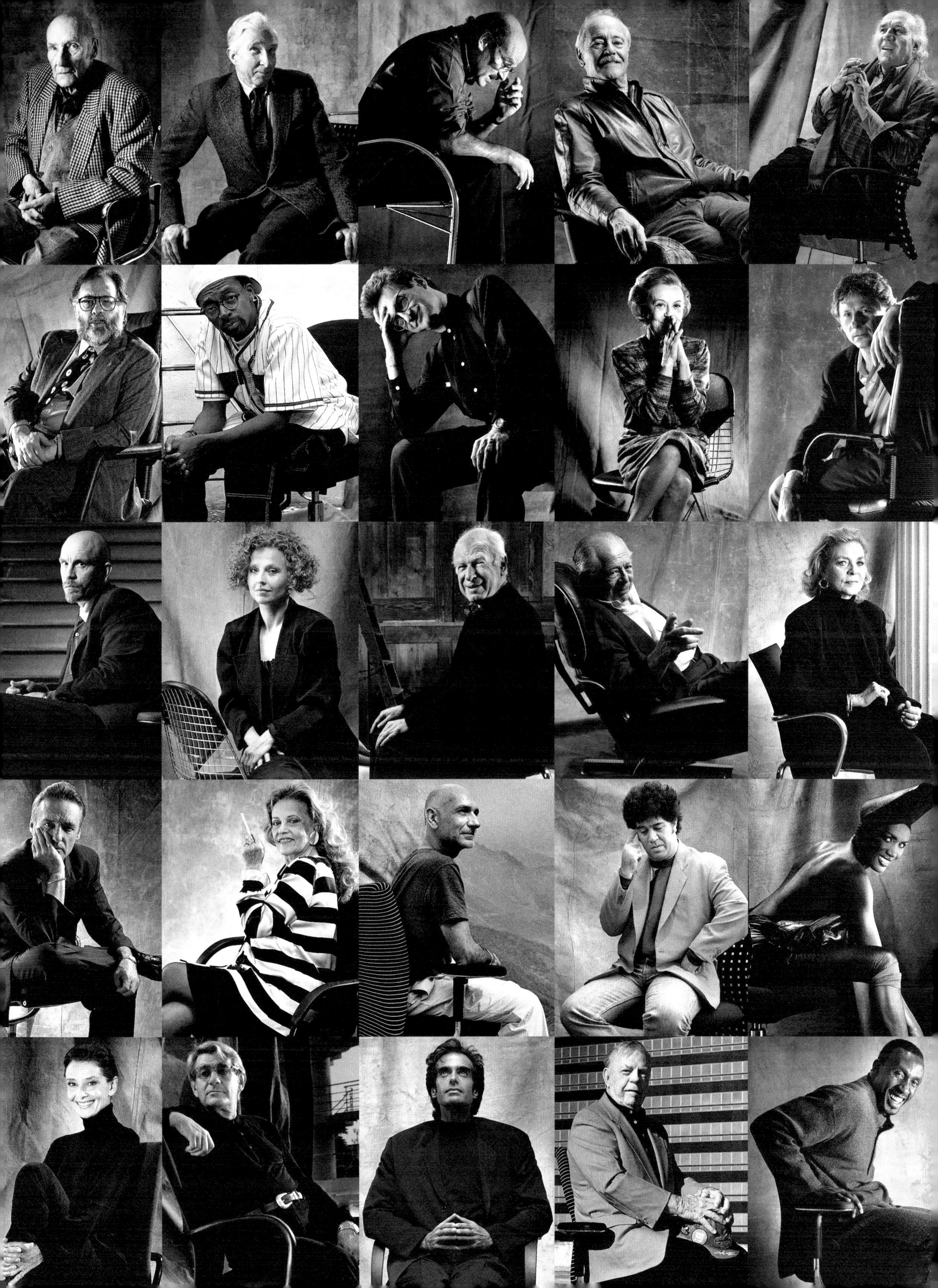

Barbara Hendricks
soprano, on Soft Pad Chair
Design: Charles and
Ray Eames

Giorgio Giugiaro
Designer, on AC 2
Design: Antonio Citterio

Jean Marais
actor, on Imago
Design: Mario Bellini with
Dieter Thiel

Daniel Barenboim
conductor and pianist,
on Lounge Chair
Design: Charles and
Ray Eames

Ali Akbar Khan
musician, on Figura
Design: Mario Bellini with
Dieter Thiel

George Segal,
artist, on Visavis
Design: Antonio Citterio

Milos Forman
film director, on Figura II
Design: Mario Bellini with
Dieter Thiel

Ringo Starr
musician, on AC 2
Design: Antonio Citterio

Doug Tompkins
project director,
former creative director of
Esprit, on Persona
Design: Mario Bellini with
Dieter Thiel

Robert Rauschenberg
painter,
on How High The Moon
Design: Shiro Kuramata

Giorgio Strehler
theater director,
on Soft Pad Chair
Design: Charles and
Ray Eames

Tomi Ungerer
artist, on AC 1
Design: Antonio Citterio

Jerry Lewis
actor, on T-Chair
Design: Antonio Citterio with
Glen Oliver Löw

John Baldessari
artist, on Figura II
Design: Mario Bellini with
Dieter Thiel

Leo Castelli
art dealer, on AC 1
Design: Antonio Citterio

Ed Koch
former mayor of New York,
on AC 2
Design: Antonio Citterio

Julia Migenes
singer and dancer, on Onda
Design: Mario Bellini with
Dieter Thiel

Isabelle Huppert
actress, on Aluminium Chair
Design: Charles and
Ray Eames

Victor Korchnoi
chess grandmaster,
on Lobby Chair
Design: Charles and
Ray Eames

John Irving
author, on AC 3
Design: Antonio Citterio

Alain Delon
actor, on Aluminium Chair
Design: Charles and
Ray Eames

Simon Estes
opera singer (bass-baritone),
on Soft Pad Chair
Design: Charles and
Ray Eames

Luciano Benetton
entrepreneur, on AC 2
Design: Antonio Citterio

Alexandre Trauner
film designer,
on Aluminium Chair
Design: Charles and
Ray Eames

Garry Kasparov
chess world champion,
on Persona
Design: Mario Bellini with
Dieter Thiel

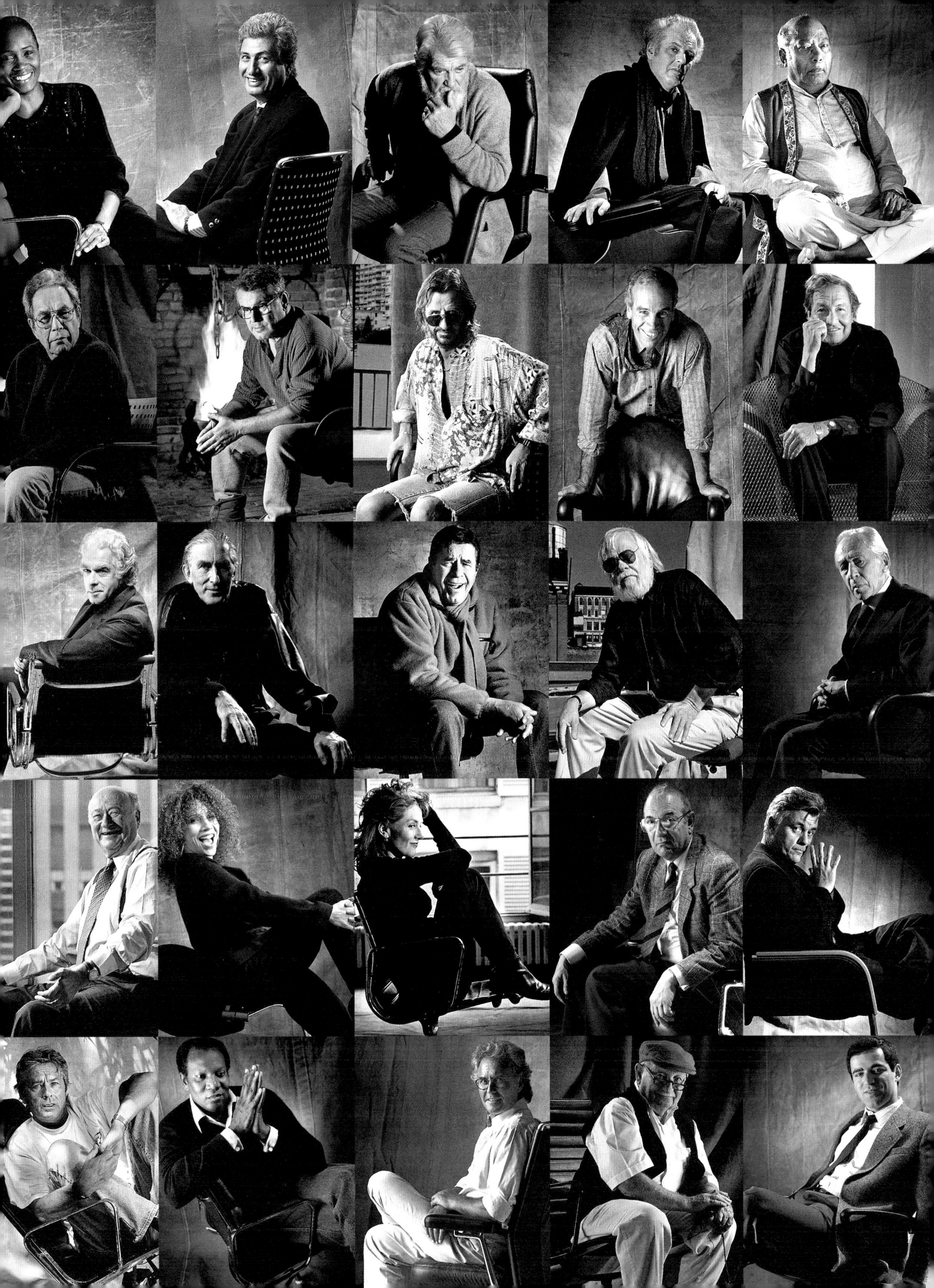

Oleg Popov
clown, on Soft Pad Chair
Design: Charles and
Ray Eames

Zino Davidoff
Havana expert,
on Lounge Chair
Design: Charles and
Ray Eames

Antonio Gades
dancer and choreographer,
on Figura
Design: Mario Bellini with
Dieter Thiel

Gil Evans
jazz musician, on Figura
Design: Mario Bellini with
Dieter Thiel

Phil Collins
musician, on Louis 20
Design: Philippe Starck

Sting
musician, on Soft Pad Chair
Design: Charles and
Ray Eames

Philip Glass,
composer, on AC 2
Design: Antonio Citterio

Yehudi Menuhin
violinist and conductor,
on Persona
Design: Mario Bellini with
Dieter Thiel

Daniel Spoerri
artist, on AC 1
Design: Antonio Citterio

Vaclav Havel
statesman, on Sedlak
Design: Borek Sipek

Claes Oldenburg
sculptor, and
Coosje van Bruggen,
author, on Eames Chaise
Design: Charles and
Ray Eames

Hugo Pratt
cartoonist, on Louis 20
Design: Philippe Starck

Jan Hoet
museum director and head of
Documenta 1992,
on Ply-Chair
Design: Jasper Morrison

Reinhold Messner
mountaineer and author,
on Onda
Design: Mario Bellini with
Dieter Thiel

Antoni Tàpies
painter, on Aluminium Chair
Design: Charles and
Ray Eames

Barbara Kruger
artist, on Louis 20
Design: Philippe Starck

Kronos Quartet
musicians, on Louis 20
and table Louise
Design: Philippe Starck

Margarete Mitscherlich
psychologist and author,
on Aluminium Chair
Design: Charles and
Ray Eames

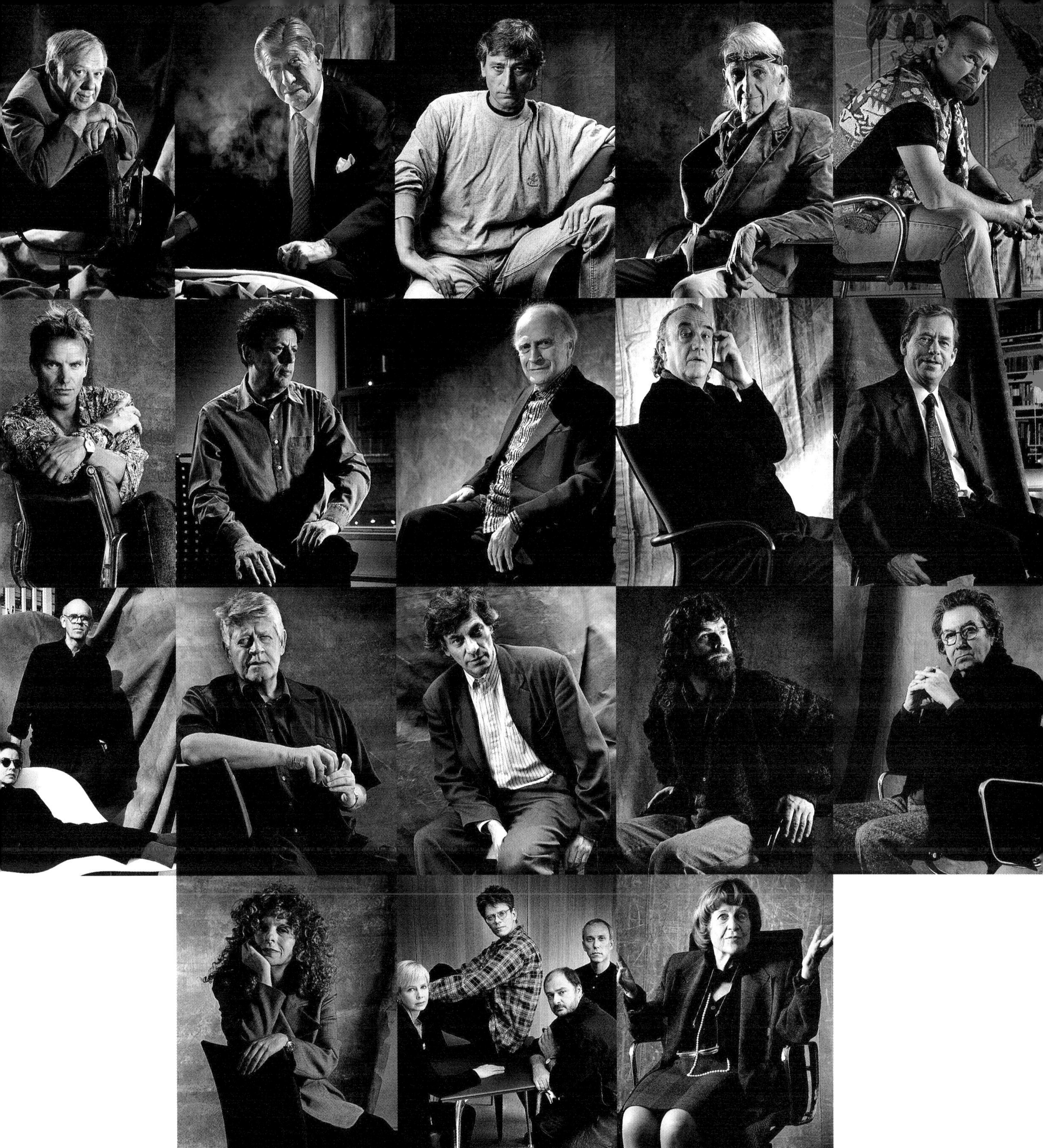

Prestel Verlag
Mandlstrasse 26
80802 Munich, Germany
Tel. +49 (89) 38 17 09-0
Fax +49 (89) 38 17 09-35

4 Bloomsbury Place
London WC1A 2QA
Tel. +44 (20) 7323-5004
Fax +44 (20) 7636-8004

175 Fifth Avenue
Suite 402
New York, NY 10010
Tel. (212) 995-2720
Fax (212) 995-2733

www.prestel.com

Prestel books are available worldwide.

Please contact your nearest bookseller or write to any of our addresses for information concerning your local distributor.

Very special thanks to Carol Diehl, who organized all the photo sessions

Designed by ADN Switzerland, Werner Jeker, and Ramón López
Lithography: ReproLine, Munich
Paper: Nopacoat Prestige 200g/m²
Printed by Sellier, Freising
Bound by Conzella, Pfarrkirchen

Printed in Germany
on acid-free paper

ISBN 3-7913-2482-9